'sooner'

A Season as Lived and Played by Tinker Owens

Text by
BILL BRUNS

Photographs by
RICH CLARKSON

First Printing . . . August, 1974
© 1974, By
JOSTEN'S PUBLICATIONS
4000 Adams Street
Topeka, Kansas 66609

Library of Congress
Catalog Card Number: 74-12784
Printed in the United States of America

CONTENTS

CHAPTER I THE GOOD OL' BOYS

"You reckon they can tell I'm the Okie from Muskogee?"

OLEN OWENS,
at the Heisman Trophy banquet, 1969

The fantasy of most young boys growing up in Oklahoma is to one day play football for the University of Oklahoma. But the highest compliment is to one day be called a "good ol' boy."

"That's someone with a good personality, a guy who likes to drink his beer and get in a little trouble, but have the knowhow to get out," says Olen Owens. "I'm 57 years old and I never was in jail in my life. I knew when to leave."

Although failing health has forced Olen into early retirement from the hell-raising circuit, seven sons carry on the tradition. "I guess it's hereditary," says Charles "Tinker" Owens, the family's second youngest, and a football hero for the Oklahoma Sooners.

On a mid-August afternoon in 1973, as Tinker packed his bags for his sophomore year down in Norman, Olen leaned back in his living room recliner and remembered the night when another son, Paul, got out of the Navy.

"He called me collect from a bar in Long Beach, California. We were talking and I could tell he was having a few beers. But then I couldn't hear him. I could hear the juke box and lots of noise in the background but old Paul, he just passed out right there in the booth.

"That call cost me $43, too, until someone finally hung up the phone."

The Owens family (minus daughters Della and Patsy): front row, Paul, Jimbo and Larry. Back row, Bill, Dale, Cherry, Olen, Steve and Tinker.

Miami, Oklahoma, they say, is a town where the men go out Saturday night and then try to patch themselves up in time for church on Sunday. It's a town of about 13,800, just off the Will Rogers Turnpike in the northeast corner of Oklahoma near the Kansas and Missouri borders. The "interesting events of the area," according to a Chamber of Commerce publication, are the Devil's Promenade Pow-Wow, the Seneca-Cayuga Green Corn Feast, the Spoonbill Fishathon, the Jaycee's Rodeo and the Tri-State Spook Light — "one of the phenomenons that has been observed since the beginning of Indian Territory." Miami is also where Steve Owens, the 1969 Heisman Trophy winner and Detroit Lions star, got his start.

One of these days they may get around to writing about the Owens family — Miami's answer to neighboring Commerce, which fostered Mickey Mantle in his youth. Already there are Steve Owens billboards to greet visitors at both ends of town, stationed appropriately on "Steve Owens Blvd." Discussions have been held about naming a street for Tinker Owens, too, but the feeling was, "It's too soon."

Olen Owens was raised near Muskogee, Oklahoma, and married Cherry Crews of nearby Gore in 1935. That year he started driving a truck, a job he held until he retired in 1972. "I knew every hole in the road between here and Dallas," said Olen, who moved to Miami in 1951 when his company shifted headquarters.

The family lived in several rented houses before buying their present three-bedroom home in 1956. By then, there were seven sons and two daughters. Paul had already married (and Bill and the two girls would soon do so) but for a while there were 11 people squeezed into the house; Olen's mother lived in the back porch utility room. "I don't know how we all lived here but we did," said Cherry. "It's crowded with three of us now."

"Steve still doesn't know what a table is," said Olen. "He just heads for the living room couch to eat."

Starting with Steve, the third oldest son, the Owens boys all played organized sports as soon as they were old enough.

A big, powerful running back, Steve was high school All-American in 1965 and pursued by dozens of colleges. "One morning there were three coaches in the kitchen, drinking coffee, while I tried to get the kids off to school," Cherry recalls. "Another time, seven recruiters showed up before we even ate breakfast. And others would come and stay until 10 or 11 at night."

Steve was leaning towards Arkansas because he liked their program and their recruiter, Jim Mackenzie. But when Mackenzie suddenly was named the head coach at Oklahoma, Steve decided to follow. Four years later, after a remarkable career in which he broke several collegiate rushing records, he won the Heisman Trophy as the best player in the country.

Olen and Cherry were flown to New York· for the Heisman ceremonies. As she remembers, "We kinda felt like the Beverly Hillbillies. We'd never gone anywhere before. In fact, I'd never even flown. It was the first time Olen had worn a tuxedo."

"And the last time," he said.

Tinker can't remember how he acquired his name. "I guess I always wanted to watch Pinky Lee when I was real little," he recalled, "and when my sisters would change the channel I'd start crying. I couldn't say Pinky — only Tinky — so everyone started calling me Tink or Tinker." The woman who ran the self-service laundry next door was the only person who ever called him Charles.

"I'm glad I have the name," he said. "It's easy to remember. I mean, how many Tinker's do you know? I'd damn sure rather be called Tinker than Charles. 'There's No. 11, Charles Owens running onto the field.' Doesn't that sound funny?"

Tinker, who started playing tackle on the sandlots when he was about eight, was always quick but skinny. He weighed 125 pounds as a high school sophomore — "the next to littlest guy on the team". By his senior year he had "beefed" up to 155. "I didn't have blazing speed but I got where nobody could outrun me."

Wearing Steve's No. 42 in football, Tinker followed up his brother's athletic heroics for the Miami High Wardogs. As a 5-11 senior he played halfback, defensive back and punted, returned punts and hauled back kickoffs for a team that was 10-1-1. He was a starting guard for the State 3A basketball champs, who were 27-0 for the season. In track he won the state titles in the high and low hurdles and the long jump. So it came as little surprise when he was named Oklahoma's "Prep Athlete of the Year" in 1971.

Still, the recruiters shied away — worried by his size, and by the feeling that he was set on Oklahoma. Yet he almost went to Arkansas to avoid falling into Steve's awesome shadow. Besides, the Razorbacks had a pass-oriented offense. "But the guy who recruited me coached their defensive backfield. I got the impression that's where they wanted me to play — and I wanted to be a receiver." So when the scholarship offer came through from Oklahoma, Tinker accepted, and set about to prove that he wasn't riding into school on Steve's press clippings.

Steve (below) with Tinker.

Fronting on D Street, across from a beer warehouse and near the railroad tracks, the white-framed Owens house is well-worn but spotlessly clean. A vegetable garden grows in the back of the house, but there's no room for a front yard. The wood-paneled living room walls are covered with family memorabilia — framed pictures, posters, citations — while the shelves are filled with trophies and medals, nearly all of them won by Steve, Tinker and Jimbo, a high school senior in 1973-74.

"Steve just loves to look through his old scrapbooks," said his mother. "He was looking at the pictures on the wall the last time he was here and told me, 'That was the best time of my life — those years at OU'."

Off the living room, on the way to the kitchen, is a large bedroom which Jimbo inherited when Tinker went off to Oklahoma. "It's gone all to hell," said Tinker, nodding toward rock music posters, pictures of the Beatles and two signs: "Guts" and "Do It With Gusto."

Jimbo was not one to let important family traditions die, however. He had left for pre-season football practice at 5:30 one Saturday night and didn't come home until nearly 5:30 the next morning.

"If they keep having 12-hour practices," Olen grumbled, "I figure they're going to have a hell of a team this year."

Tinker in the front room, where his pictures and awards are competing with Steve for wallspace. Jimbo is now adding to the trophy collection, but the whole family hangs in the wall gallery.

For Tinker and Terri, summer has only a few days before practice begins in Norman. They will then see each other only on football weekends and Tinker will not play with daughter Brandi until Thanksgiving.

Tinker's summer, already shortened by the early return to Oklahoma for preseason practice, was fast drawing to a close. He tried to spend as much time as possible with his fianceé, Terri Kinkead, whose family lived in a ranch-style brick house in the "suburbs" of Miami.

"The thing about Miami, nobody hardly dates around," said Tinker. "If you have a steady girl friend, you go with her it seems like forever. It's always been that way, I guess." He began dating Terri in his junior year, when she was a sophomore. Their daughter, Brandi, was born in May of Tinker's freshman year at OU. But since Tinker had only a couple of hundred dollars in the bank, they decided to wait until after his sophomore year to get married.

Tinker worked all summer on a cement crew building roads, then would spend the evenings with Terri. They watched television, took in movies, or drove up to The Ranch in Galena, Kansas, where there was live rock music. They spent weekends at Grand Lake, where Terri's father and Bill Owens had boats for water skiing.

"Miami is good for sports and all, and the school system is good," said Tinker. "But I don't think they have enough activities or places to go. Just one movie house and a drive-in."

Several weeks before leaving for Norman to begin his sophomore year, Tinker began running in the evenings at the Northeastern A & M Junior College stadium. He and Terri also drove up to Kansas City to watch the Detroit Lions play the Chiefs in an exhibition game — the first time Tinker had seen Steve play in person as a pro. In the dressing room afterwards, a professional scout told Tinker, "We've got a good scouting report going on you; don't mess it up."

Sitting in the same row as former running great Gale Sayers (in checkered shirt) Tinker and Terri watch the Detroit-Kansas City exhibition game in Arrowhead Stadium. "There's Gale Sayers!" Tinker told Terri. "He's my idol."

After the game, Tinker meets with brother Steve and Hall of Fame receiver Raymond Berry, who tried to recruit Tinker to Arkansas.

"If it's Friday or Saturday," said Tinker, "and I don't show up, my folks don't even ask, they just figure I'm still out partying." Such was the case Friday night — two days before returning to school — when he drove up to Baxter Springs, Kansas, for his "last night out" of the summer. The fun was marred only when Tinker got into a scuffle with an old high school classmate, cutting an arm on some gravel.

Saturday afternoon, before a hamburger feed at the Kinkead's, Tinker was still trying to pull himself together. But he couldn't resist throwing the football around with Terri's older brother Mark, who once played at Brigham Young.

Tinker's torso is sparse but rock-hard; to look at him — an even 6 feet tall, with average-sized hands — one must envision a big-time college coach telling him, "Kid, you'll love our intramural program." But that preconception is shattered when Tinker started catching hard-thrown passes casually, with just one hand.

"It's a matter of concentration," Tinker explained. "When you're my size, you make do with what you got. I've never had any troubles catching the ball. It more or less came naturally."

The parties of summer's end began Friday night — a night out with old high school chums at the favorite hangout in Baxter Springs.

Tinker enjoys a night of pool with Mike McVay and Max Mantle, a kinfolk of Mickey's.

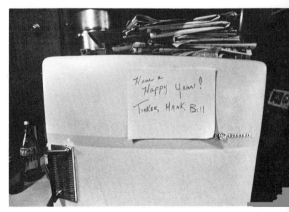

The next night, the college good-by party at the Kinkeads features football — tossed and televised, and hamburgers — barbecued and relished.

Cherry Owens serves up breakfast.

When his bags were packed — "Anybody want a free Steve Owens poster?" he asked some visitors. "I'm giving them away" — and his green 1966 Ford was ready to go. Tinker kissed his mother good bye and shook hands with his father.

"I'll call you soon," Tinker said.

"Well, if you get in jail, don't call me collect," Olen replied.

"I'll let the police call you," Tinker grinned.

Soon he was out on Interstate 44, driving down past the green, gently rolling farmlands and cattle ranches towards Tulsa and Oklahoma City. "I'm really excited to come back," he said. "I'm a lot more confident of myself this year and I think we're going to have a good season."

A year earlier when he drove the 180 miles down to Norman, he didn't think he was good enough to make the varsity squad, even though freshmen were eligible to play for the first time since the Korean War. "I was bothered by my size 'cause I wasn't that big and I figured I'd have to grow a little bit. I was worried I would mess up and not do any good. People were talking about how I was too small to play football in college. They figured the only reason I got a scholarship was because of Steve."

Tinker underestimated his other assets as a receiver, such as his quick-starting 4.6 speed ("4.5 with a tailwind"), his sure hands and his competitive grit. In pre-season practices he ran his patterns so well that he was consistently beating the varsity defensive backs. "He proved he was more than Steve's little brother," safety Randy Hughes recalls. Finally coach Chuck Fairbanks activated Tinker for the second varsity game of the season against Oregon. He told him to see equipment manager Jack Baer for a number.

"We ain't got no damn numbers," Baer told Tinker.

"Surely some guy's hurt," Tinker said tentatively.

Baer studied his roster. "Well, what number do you want, 63 or 11?"

"I think I'll take No. 11," Tinker replied, thus passing up his chance to become an offensive guard.

Saturday afternoon, Tinker was sitting on the bench, enjoying the game, when John Carroll, the first-team wide receiver, came off the field with a knee injury.

Tinker remembers, "I heard a coach call, 'Tinker Owens, Tinker Owens.' When I ran out on the field, nobody knew who I was — not even the PA announcer — 'cause my name wasn't in the program. No. 11 belonged to an injured quarterback. I was the mystery man, the phantom receiver."

Tinker caught two passes for 18 yards, and the following week against Clemson he was in the starting lineup. "Here I was, I had been with the varsity a week and three days and I was starting on the Oklahoma football team, which is really a dream come true for almost every little kid in Oklahoma."

When Carroll returned to the lineup, Tinker moved back to the bench. Then

Carroll limped off for good in the second quarter against Nebraska, in a late November showdown game for the Sugar Bowl invitation.

Nebraska led at halftime, 7-0, and Tinker told Fairbanks, "My man has been going for every fake and I've beaten him on every play." So when Oklahoma fell behind, 14-0, Fairbanks told quarterback Dave Robertson to put the ball in the air. "And don't forget Owens." Tinker responded with five clutch receptions that helped set up two touchdowns and the game winning field goal as the Sooners stormed back to win, 17-14. Afterwards, when Tinker stepped aboard the team bus, his teammates applauded and started yelling "Star . . . Hero . . . Super Frosh."

Capping his remarkable yearling season, the "phantom receiver" won Most Valuable Player honors in the Sugar Bowl victory over Penn State in New Orleans. He caught one touchdown pass and set up another with an acrobatic grab at the 1-yard line as Oklahoma won, 14-0.

At 4 a.m. the next morning — still out celebrating — Tinker and Steve decided to call home and wish their parents a Happy New Year. "Did we get you up?" Tinker asked.

Despite his sudden fame — a fan club had even been organized, and a rancher would name his bull Tinker Owens II — Tinker was still a small-town Oklahoma boy at heart. Before leaving New Orleans he went out to dinner at Brennan's with a magazine photographer. The photographer ordered a fine Beaujolais, but after taking a couple of sips, Tinker motioned for the wine steward.

"Uh, this wine . . . " he whispered. The steward bent closer. "Do you have any Boone's Farm Strawberry Hill?"

Shopping for school clothes, Tinker tries on a hat at The Hub, a Miami men's store, "where most guys shop," said Tinker. He decided he didn't really need a hat to go with his four new pair of Levis.

Out in front of Terri's house the day before leaving for Norman, Tinker recounts the previous night's partying. He talks with Hank Hecksher and Bill Mahan, friends of Terri's family.

Tinker packs his car in front of the Owens home.

After New Orleans, it was a tumultuous off-season for Tinker Owens and the Oklahoma football program.

In January, 1973, Chuck Fairbanks suddenly signed as head coach of the New England Patriots, and his offensive coordinator, 35-year-old Barry Switzer, was named as his successor.

Then one day signs started appearing on campus announcing the Tinker Owens Laundromat. It was supposed to be located at Heisman Square, where Steve owned a sporting goods store. Soon after that leaflets were distributed touting a free box of "Tinker's Touchdown Soap" for so many pounds of laundry. All of which is illegal for a college football player. Tinker finally tracked down the culprit — an OU coed who was trying to wrangle a date — but the Big 8 still sent an investigator to poke around and confirm the hoax.

In April, however, a scandal broke that wasn't a practical joke, and Oklahoma was axed down by the Big 8 and the NCAA.

During spring practice the Sooners turned themselves in, announcing that high school transcripts had been altered for starting quarterback Kerry Jackson and back up center Mike Phillips so that they could enter Oklahoma on athletic scholarships. Joe Woolley, head football coach at Ball High School in Galveston, Texas, admitted falsifying their class standings — but with the knowledge of an OU assistant coach.

Jackson, a fine runner with a great passing arm, who was being counted on as Oklahoma's starting quarterback, was subsequently ruled ineligible for 1973. But then came the crusher: Oklahoma was put on two years probation, meaning no bowl games in 1973 or 1974, and no national

TV appearances in 1974-75.

When Switzer learned the news at an NCAA meeting in Chicago, he came out with tears in his eyes. "The only thing to do now is fight," he said. "Rise and face the challenge." Several days later he received a telegram from his players: "Coach, we came to the University of Oklahoma to play for a champion. They can't change that. We accept the challenge."

"We'll have to live with the probation," said Tinker, on the drive down to Norman for the start of 1973 practice. "But I'm real happy about Switzer. He'll have a better relationship with the players. You never saw coach Fairbanks kidding around. He was Mr. Serious all the time. But coach Switzer says things in a meeting or out on the field to make you laugh. He's real serious about winning, you know, but he keeps it loose.

"He's young, too, and he knows we're going to go out and party a little. He knows we're not going to sit around the dorm all the time and study."

CHAPTER 2 •I-35•

"The greatest reward in football is winning. That's the most important goal there is. That's why they have scoreboards."

BARRY SWITZER,
greeting the 1973 team

The football dorm at Oklahoma is a four-story, red-brick building, located a couple of deep pass patterns from Owen Stadium, the football dressing room, and O'Connell's Irish Pub. Built in the late 1940's the dorm has since been humbled by the country-club comfort at other universities, so a new structure is being planned.

When Tinker arrived in mid-afternoon, his new roommate, 188-pound freshman quarterback Joe McReynolds, was already there, his bags still unpacked except for large economy size jars of Vitamin C and Zest Tabs on one shelf. The air conditioned room was large enough for a bunk bed, a closet, a joint desk, a telephone and Oklahoma-red carpeting. Television sets were not allowed in individual rooms. Tinker plugged in his clock radio and hung the obligatory Schlitz beer clock that glows in the dark.

McReynolds grew up in Purcell, 18 miles south of Norman, where he succeeded Tinker as Oklahoma's "Prep Athlete of the Year." Steve Owens, in fact, helped recruit Joe, but Texas A&M had the inside line. "I called A&M and told them I was going to sign with them," Joe recalled. "But the next morning coach Harper (of Oklahoma) was at my door. We went to dinner that night and he talked me into OU. It's a once-in-a-lifetime opportunity to get a scholarship from OU. It's something you just can't turn down if you're an Oklahoma boy."

Tinker agreed. "I was thinking about Arkansas. But when it came right down to it, I only wanted to go to Oklahoma. I didn't want to go out of state. And I couldn't go to Oklahoma State. I was afraid Steve might kill me. He said he would."

There was still an hour before the players had to report for their weigh-ins. "Let's go to McDonald's," Joe suggested. "I want to weigh 190."

Three hours later, he unloads at the athletic dorm.

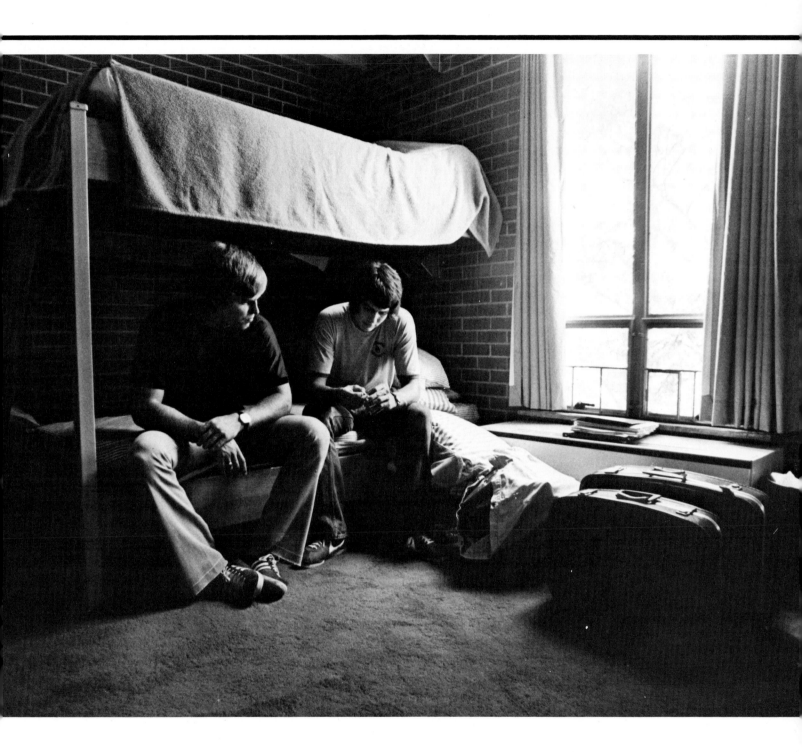

Oklahoma's football team goes through the chow line at the traditional welcome back picnic in Owen Stadium.

Tinker gets re-acquainted (below) with Steve Davis, who would be the Sooner quarterback. Davis was a licensed Baptist minister, but without a church.

Walking over to the football dressing room, which is tucked under the west stands of Owen Field, Tinker told Joe, "I don't know why they want to weigh me. They know I'm going to come back skinny anyway."

All players were assigned a weight when they went home for summer, a rule designed mainly for linemen. Thus, the 230 pounders are kept from ballooning to 275 unless, of course, they are working with weights.

Assistant coach Jerry Pettibone was running the scales at the weigh-in. Tinker climbed on and Pettibone announced, "Tinker Owens mashes the scales at ... 166." Tinker grinned. "I came back the same, coach," he said. He would be the lightest player on the team.

A couple of hours later, players and coaches mingled with OU administrators and faculty members at the traditional fried chicken picnic in the stadium. There were jokes about it being "the Last Supper" before three-a-day practices, to which Tinker added, "Down at Arkansas they call this the feedin' before the hog killin'."

Afterwards, coach Switzer said a few words. He reminded the players, "We have one of the finest football traditions in the country. But you all know that — you were told that by your recruiters." Then he introduced school president Paul Sharp as, "The *real* head coach at Oklahoma University."

Sharp seemed pleased. "I've never been introduced as head coach before," he said, "And I've never diagnosed a play for you."

"Just keep doing that!" Switzer shot back. They both laughed, and Sharp countered, "Well, as we say in this state — win or tie."

Oklahoma president Paul Sharp and head coach Barry Switzer swap jokes while greeting the players.

Tinker at the weigh-in: "I don't know why they want to weigh me. I guess they just want to laugh." From left, coaches Jerry Pettibone, Warren Harper and Gene Hochevar.

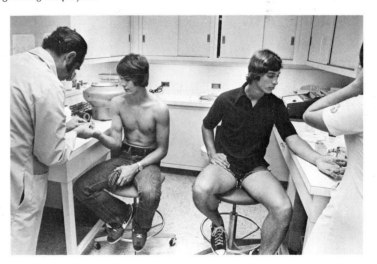

Going through the physical check-up, Tinker and Doug Pearson have their blood checked. Pearson was a third team receiver from Pryor, Oklahoma, and one of Tinker's best friends.

Tinker stands with legs crossed and hands behind his head — "to get my air back."

Monday afternoon, in 90-degree heat and exhausting humidity, the Sooners came out in freshly laundered T-shirts and shorts but they straggled back to the dressing room 45 minutes later with those sweat soaked T-shirts tied around their heads or waists. The workout started with a mile run, followed by calisthenics and stretching exercises. It finished with a series of gut-busting sprints at 90, 220 and 440 yards. "I can run 'em," wheezed Tinker, working hard from the start. "I just don't know how fast."

Struggling for air while roommate McReynolds was bent in pain, Tinker later said, "I was tired but I thought Joe was going to die."

The Sooners run a mile, the first salvo of pre-season practice.

Switzer studies his team's conditioning.

Pinned on a wall in the coaching offices is a daily, updated depth chart, ranking the players at each position. Below that, under the heading "I-35," is a list of those players who have quit the team and started for home, in most cases out onto I-35, which runs between Oklahoma City and Dallas. Less than a dozen players would "I-35" the first two weeks of practice. "But everybody talks about it," said Jimbo Elrod, Tinker's good friend and a 208-pound linebacker who was being converted to defensive end.

"Coach Lacewell will come down the hall in the morning," said Elrod, "pounding on the doors to wake us up, shouting, 'You've got to love it! You've got to give it all to the Big Red!' And you're thinking, 'What in the hell am I doing here?'"

Monday's initial workout simply tightened up the muscles for the agony of three-a-day practices Tuesday, Wednesday and Thursday, before the players were allowed to wear full uniforms. First came the wakeup at 6:45, then orange juice and salt tablets in the dressing room and practice at 7:30 . . . breakfast and a nap . . . a workout at noon in 95-degree heat . . . lunch and another nap or plain relaxing before the final practice at 6:45. After dinner there wasn't much time, or spirit, to do much more than go to bed.

"If you tried to stay out late and drink beer, there's no way you'd make it the next morning," said Tinker. His late summer running program had helped — but nothing prepares the body for that painful transition into football-fit condition. "Your whole body gets fatigued," he said. "You're just going all day, running plays over and over, and it's so hot it just drains you." One player hadn't run a day all summer. Tinker had no sympathy for him when he collapsed. "Hell, he deserved it."

Joe McReynolds, for example, had worked out every day throughout the summer, including two-a-day workouts for the two weeks leading up to the Oil Bowl All-Star game that featured the state's finest prep graduates versus Texas' best. The Oil Bowl had been played on Saturday. Now, Tuesday night, Joe sprawled out in the dorm room with his roommate of two days and groaned, "I've never hurt so much in my life as I did today."

As practices progressed, something was added to the sprints: helmets.

A grinning Switzer leads the traditional charge as Clyde Powers trips and falls.

Tinker displays his hurdling skill for an unconvinced photographer.

Picture Day has been a tradition at Oklahoma since 1930. It gives the newspaper photographers a chance to stock their files. Television crews and radio interviewers produce a week's worth of features. Plus there is always a father or two, armed with a Rolleiflex, who manages to slip onto the field to pose his sons with an Oklahoma player, like Tinker.

Another highlight comes when the Oklahoma team, freshly suited up in game uniforms, charges symbolically onto the field for TV cameras and the 6 o'clock news.

This day, the head coach led the way as the Sooners started their rush like a stampede of Merrill Lynch bulls, only to have cornerback Clyde Powers trip and fall to the turf. The Sooners had to regroup and come charging out a second time.

Later, a newspaper photographer, lying prone on the grass, tried several times to get Tinker to leap in the air as he ran with the ball. "You're not a very good hurdler," the photographer grumbled. "I was *only* state champ in the hurdles," Tinker muttered under his breath.

During the interviews, a television reporter asked Tinker how he handicapped the Big 8 football race. He hedged, refusing to name a favorite. Later he explained, "Questions like that really put you on the spot. You want to be honest but you don't want to say, 'Well, we're the best' because that will get around to the other teams, and it just gives them more incentive." He was still reconciling the fact that athletes have to learn to play it "safe", to talk casually with the news media without really saying anything — which means boring interviews but contented football coaches.

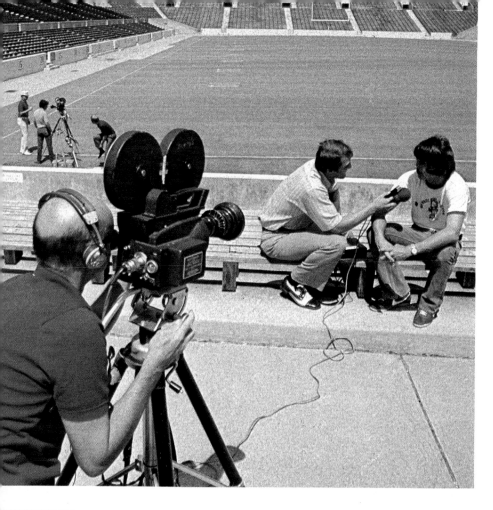

A carefree Tinker was being careful about his pre-season predictions as he was interviewed on television (above left), by newspaper reporters, and on radio (above).

Offensive coordinator Galen Hall addresses his players the second day.

In Switzer's view, the mental conditioning of his players was as important as their physical preparations. Thus there were daily meetings throughout the preseason drills, either as a team, as an offense or defense, or as individual units (receivers, linebackers, and so on).

Oklahoma's new offensive coordinator was 33-year-old Galen Hall, who quarterbacked Penn State to three straight bowl games, played two years for the Washington Redskins and New York Jets, then opted for a coaching career. He joined the Sooner staff in 1966, the same year as Switzer, and has since acquired a comfortable stomach and a reputation for possessing one of the shrewdest offensive minds in college football.

"We lost eight offensive starters," Hall told his offense in their first meeting together. "We've got a great challenge ahead of us. We have enough physical talent in this room to meet that challenge. But the players we lost had a great mental understanding of the Wishbone (the Oklahoma offense). This is the thing I'm worried about now: how much mental attention you're going to give us. The physical attention, we'll get. What we need now is your undivided mental attention for about 10 days, through two-a-days."

For those who lasted, the two-a-day drills would end on the day classes began.

Drained by the heat and early practices, Tinker struggles to stay awake.

The Sooners would meet in specialized units (such as the receivers, above) or as a team, listening to Switzer's opening-night speech (below).

Tinker, wearing an unfamiliar No. 7, sharpens his pass catching skills while receiver coach Don Duncan looks on.

Don Duncan, the 32-year-old receiver coach, was in his first year at Oklahoma, having stepped up from the head coaching job at Navarro Junior College in Texas. He also brought along a receiver named Billy Brooks, who just happened to be 6-3, 200 pounds with enormous hands and 9.6 speed in the 100 — the kind of athlete Oklahoma seldom rejects.

Unfortunately, the Sooners' Wishbone offense allowed for only one wide receiver — and that was Tinker Owens. Brooks would be tried at tight end, where first-stringer John Carroll was still hobbling on a bad knee.

Most schools run offenses that would capitalize on Owens and Brooks as wide receivers on opposite sides of the field. But nobody had Oklahoma's overpowering rushing game. The Sooners stressed a running attack in which the quarterback has to run the option and pass — in that order of importance. The year before they had averaged 338 yards a game on the ground compared to 100 yards passing.

"I've never been convinced that you can win consistently passing the ball," said Switzer. "If you can't move the ball on the ground, it is very difficult to maintain an effective attack. I don't think you'll ever win a national championship throwing 40 times a game."

After losing their one-man offense when Steve Owens graduated in 1969, the Sooners converted to the Wishbone in a desperate gamble early in the 1970 season. The glory years of Bud Wilkinson, who had brought Oklahoma football to national prominence, had finally run their course with 7-4 and 6-4 records in 1968 and 1969.

When Oklahoma opened 1970 with two mediocre wins and an upset loss to Oregon State, Chuck Fairbanks, coach at the time, scuttled his Veer-option formation in favor of the Wishbone, which had been introduced with devastating success by Texas. The Sooners lost to Texas two weeks later, 41-9, but finished the season with a 7-4-1 record and a bowl tie with Alabama. In 1971 and 1972, they finished with consecutive No. 2 rankings in the country.

"The Wishbone is why Fairbanks is in the pros, Switzer is head coach, and I'm his offensive coordinator," said Galen Hall. "Otherwise we would have all lost our jobs."

Duncan discusses pass routes with his receivers.

Tinker and receivers practice coming off the scrimmage line at top speed for five or six steps.

Players have their ankles taped before practice in Ken Rawlinson's training room.

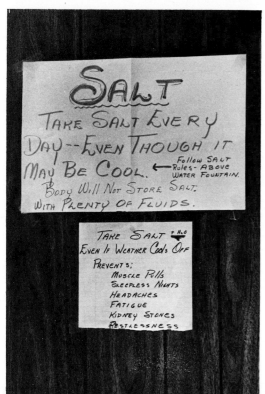

When Don Duncan first met with the pass catchers, he told them, "I want you to be smart receivers. Practice will be a lot of running, a lot of pass catching and a lot of repetition until you become sick of it. But it becomes second nature and it will make the difference."

The trouble was to coordinate their pass routes with sophomore quarterback Steve Davis, who had won the job after Kerry Jackson's ineligibility. Neither Davis nor back-up Scott Hill, in fact, had ever played a minute of college football.

Tinker spent nearly three frustrating weeks trying to reach harmony with Davis' passes. "I go out for a pass and I turn around and it hits me in the leg or something," he said after the first week. "I won't even see it coming." A week before the season opener against Baylor the situation had improved — a little. "Steve's throwing the ball real well," he recalled, "but his timing's so bad you run out of bounds trying to catch it, or it's behind you or something. When he has you go out for a pass you can't tell where it's going for sure."

Meanwhile, Tinker was depressed by a troublesome off-field development — the start of classes. It was an event he accepted with mixed blessings: it meant the end of two-a-day practices, only to be replaced by morning classes, an activity which ranked well below football, Terri, his family, partying and playing Crazy 8's.

"I've never been ready to start school," he said. "Something about the summer, leisuring around, then to come back and trying to study while playing football. But it's something you have to make yourself do. They just don't give you the grades."

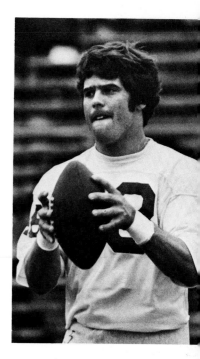

Quarterback Steve Davis

Tinker and Mike Phillips enjoy a Gatorade-popsicle break during a mid-day practice.

Two weeks into practice, as the Sooners struggled to piece together their passing attack, Tinker was injured in a Sunday scrimmage. "I ran a curl pattern but Steve Davis threw the ball behind me," he recalled. "When I reached back I caught it but was sandwiched by the corner and safety. I lost my breath, and found out I had a deep bruise on my back. I had trouble sleeping on Sunday night. Was in quite a bit of pain."

When Tinker returned to practice, the opener with Baylor was only a week away. But the Sooner offense, plagued by mistakes and fumbles and trying to incorporate the eight new starters, was finally starting to fit together.

"Practice was the best the offense has had since we started," Tinker wrote in his notebook on Monday. "QB's passing better than before. Mind really on Baylor now more than before. Can't wait till game night." On Thursday he added: "We had a great practice. We ran 30 pass plays against the expected Baylor defenses, just going through the formations, and only two were incomplete."

All summer there had been far less worries about the Oklahoma defense, an experienced unit which Switzer felt could be the best in the country. He had All-American candidates in defensive end Gary Baccus, linebacker Rod Shoate, safety Randy Hughes and cornerback Kenith Pope, and the remarkable Selmon brothers — Lucious (5-11, 232), Dewey (6-1, 249) and LeRoy (6-2, 252). The Selmons, who grew up on a small farm in Eufaula, Oklahoma, would now line up together on the defensive line.

Then, a week before practice began, LeRoy was hospitalized by pericarditis, a viral infection of the sac surrounding the heart. The Sooners were told he would be sidelined for at least six to eight weeks or perhaps the season. Two weeks after that, another shock went through the Sooners — the doctors wanted to run tests on Lucious and Dewey, fearing that LeRoy's illness might be hereditary. That was the low point for an already embattled team.

Spirits soared three days later, however, when all three Selmons came into the dressing room, cleared for football (LeRoy, though, had to be held out until the fourth game).

Through all the troubles, before he had even coached his first game, Switzer maintained his usual blend of intensity, self-confidence and sense of humor. "I think I'll red-shirt everybody and wait until next year," he joked one day.

He also tried to turn the setbacks into psychological advantages. The first night back on campus he told his players, "I've been to 11 bowl games in 13 seasons. I've been around a lot of success, a lot of great players. Bowl games and playing on TV are fine incentives. But I'll tell you what, people — the greatest reward in football is winning. That's the most important goal there is. That's why they have scoreboards. So when they put us on probation they made one mistake. They didn't tell us we couldn't win the Big 8 championship. And nobody said we couldn't win the national championship."

Switzer paused, looking out at his players, straight in their eyes. "Men," he said, "that is our challenge."

CHAPTER 3 HOW GOOD ?

" ... With Kerry Jackson, this Sooner Wishbone would have been devastating. Without him, Oklahoma may have to bone up on some wishes."

Magazine Clip,
Taped in Steve Davis' locker

Normally, Baylor would be a cream-puff opener for Oklahoma, a scrimmage to sharpen the Sooners for their clash with No. 1 ranked Southern Cal in two weeks. But Baylor was playing at home in Waco, Texas — "This is their bowl game," Switzer warned — with a team that reportedly could challenge Texas for the Southwest Conference title. "The coaches really had us believing that Baylor could beat us," Tinker admitted later.

Outfitted in $90 worth of slacks, shoes, shirt and tie to match his Oklahoma-red team blazer, Tinker flew with the Sooners to Waco on Friday. That night, he spoke about the pressures that were building up:

"You've been watching films, practicing, and always thinking, 'I wish Game Day would get here. Practices are killing me.' But finally you wake up and the game's there and you don't think back about all the practices you've had. You just think about the game."

"I get so high for a game it's really unbelievable. There's never been a game of football that I wasn't ready to play. I don't really have to do anything special. I just love to play football."

Since the game was at night, the Sooners had to kill the day, trying to relax. Tinker and Billy Brooks, his roommate on road trips, laid around their hotel room, trying to sleep or watch television. Tinker was unusually withdrawn and serious, with none of the kibitzing that is his nature. "The whole day I'm just thinking about the game," he said. "Things keep going through my head — pass patterns, the defenses, blocking assignments. Then when we run out on the field and I hear the people hollering and cheering, and the band starts playing 'Boomer Sooner,' I just get chills in my body. Surely is a great feeling."

"I think we've got enough good players to have a real good season," said Tinker. "But we don't really know for sure. Myself, I hope we just get our passing game together. That's what I'm really concerned about. I'm looking forward to a good season. I just hope it turns out that way."

Oklahoma had been ranked No. 15 by *Sports Illustrated* in its pre-season survey, while four opponents — Texas, Southern Cal, Colorado & Nebraska were all in the top 12. "I think we have a better team than people give us credit for," Tinker said. "We'll just have to show them tonight."

Tinker and his Oklahoma teammates come up the ramp to the field for their season opener against Baylor.

Tinker waits tensely in the locker room before the game.

Before his first game as head coach, Switzer huddles with his team moments before the kickoff. "Cut, slash, hit and have fun," he told them.

Most of the suspicions about Oklahoma's football team were washed away in the first half against Baylor. The Sooners rolled up a 35-0 margin, which led Baylor coach Grant Teaff to moan later, "They whipped us every way a team can."

Oklahoma's offensive line, maligned during pre-season practices and driven by their coaches, thoroughly dominated Baylor up front, and the Sooner backs zipped through gaping holes to gain 480 yards. Such was Oklahoma's depth that when halfback Grant Burget injured his knee, junior college transfer Waymon Clark stepped in and rumbled for 113 yards in 11 carries. But the most dazzling back on the field was Joe Washington, a 5-10, 174-pound sophomore. In shoes painted silver, trimmed in red and coated with gloss, Washington ran for 113 yards on 14 tries and scored two touchdowns. "He was absolutely phenomenal," raved Texas coach Darrell Royal, who scouted the game. "He has the best acceleration I've seen."

Quarterback Steve Davis proved that he could direct the Wishbone attack — gaining 110 yards on the ground — but the passing game was tentative at best. He tried only six passes, completing three. One of them went to Owens for 14 yards. "We could have beat them all night passing," said Tinker, "but we didn't have to. We just ran right over them." On one post pattern over the middle, he had his defender beat by five steps, but Davis overthrew him.

Afterward, Switzer explained his philosophy about the running game: "We thought the game had to be won with an assaulting type of running attack. We had to have success running right at 'em without having to throw the ball. I've always believed that you must first have success in the running game and then you worry

Tinker's first "gain" of the season came on a 15-yard penalty, indicated by the referee. Penalty aided touchdown drive.

about throwing the ball."

By halftime the tension on the Oklahoma team had slipped away and the preseason troubles were forgotten. The postgame celebration of the 42-13 triumph was, by comparison, anti-climactic.

"We can't really feel we beat a powerhouse, 'cause we didn't," Tinker cautioned. "But it gives us a lot more confidence about our team."

Although Waymon Clark proved that he could hold the job, the loss of Grant Burget tempered the victory celebration. Burget had broken a 23-yard run in the first quarter, only to catch an opponent's helmet in his knee. He tried to stay in the game. "It'll work out," he said hopefully. But when it collapsed again on the next play, he had to be helped off the field. Orthopedic specialist Dr. Don

O'Donoghue, who traveled with the team, examined the knee and Burget could see it flopping about when it should have been firm. Burget's first thought was, "I'm history," But he still held out hope that he wouldn't need a season-ending operation.

The next morning, back in Norman, O'Donoghue took another look at the knee and shook his head. He looked up and said, "Did you bring your toothbrush?"

"At least give me a day to think about it," Burget pleaded. So the doctor postponed the operation until Monday morning.

Oklahoma's 42-13 victory produced locker room jubilation, especially for Switzer to whom the team gave the game ball.

41

Heavy rains forced Oklahoma to work out in the field house (below) before the Southern Cal game in Los Angeles.

By Tuesday, Baylor had been put aside and the focus was now on Southern Cal, the defending national champs who had beaten Arkansas in their opener, 17-0. Oklahoma had an open date before the trip to Los Angeles, so Tinker was able to drive home for the first time since football practice began. He arrived for the last half of Jimbo's game and went out afterward with Terri. Saturday afternoon he watched football at her house and that night they drove to Joplin, Missouri, for a Mexican dinner.

Southern Cal whipped Georgia Tech

Soon after arriving at their hotel, the Sooners were taken on a tour of Universal City.

that day, 23-6, as expected, but Texas — which had been ranked No. 1 by *Sports Illustrated* — was upset by the University of Miami, 20-15. Oklahoma, which would play Miami and Texas following the Southern Cal game, suddenly didn't have a "breather" to look forward to in the first half of the season.

When the Sooners resumed their preparations for Southern Cal, Tinker complained, "We had a poor practice (Monday) compared to the others we had so far. We didn't look as though we were playing the No. 1 team in the nation on Saturday night." But the next day he noted, "We had a good practice. Everyone seems ready to play."

The Sooner charter flight on Friday morning marked Tinker's first trip west of Colorado. It was a hot, smoggy day in the Los Angeles basin when the Sooners arrived but Tinker was charitable. "It was really pretty coming in on the plane. All I could see was houses and swimming pools and freeways."

He scoffed at Los Angeles newspaper stories which theorized that, since Oklahoma was ineligible for post-season play, this would be its "bowl game". "Heck, this isn't a bowl game to us," he said. "We're always playing big games, and this is just another big game."

Tinker's potential rival, Billy Brooks, remained just that. "I know I'm going to be starting so I'm not worried about the situation," Tinker explained. "If they put him in the game I'm not going to be mad or anything else 'cause he's a good athlete. He's faster than me but I don't think he runs his patterns as quick as I do, or comes off the line as quick. 'Course if he gets out in the open I'm sure he can run faster than me 'cause he's got longer strides."

Tinker laughs it up with one of the Universal television characters, who said he was a retired football coach.

The Sooners were greeted by television actor Dennis Weaver, an OU graduate, who told Tinker, "What a charge you gave me last year against Nebraska."

Oklahoma rehearses its goal-line offense in the Coliseum the night before the game, as the rest of the team simulates crowd noise.

Friday night, the Sooners worked out in the Los Angeles Coliseum. As they walked down the concrete runway to the field, Switzer asked aloud, "Is that the patter of little cleats?" He paused, then answered his own question. "No, it's probably their teeth chattering."

One Oklahoma tradition is to end the last practice before each game with a short, emotional drill. Starting on the 10-yard line, the first team offense runs three straight plays while the rest of the club claps and hollers from behind the end zone to simulate crowd noise. When the offense scores, everybody slaps hands, pounds each other on the back, and then they all run off the field together.

Saturday morning, after the team breakfast and a final review of USC game film, the Sooners faced another Saturday afternoon waiting for a night game. The hotel lobby swarmed with Oklahoma rooters. Some 8,500 of them had flown out in chartered planes. A table was set up to dispense Big Red souvenirs while "Boomer Sooner" blared away on a little record player.

Back in their room, Tinker and Brooks watched the Notre Dame-Purdue game. When halfback Art Best of Notre Dame started to sweep end to a touchdown, Tinker blurted, "Joe Washington would already be in the end zone." Later, on the ABC Prudential College Scoreboard, the very first score given was, "Central Connecticut 6, Maine 3."

"Damn," Tinker cracked, "I didn't think they could beat Maine."

Tinker and road roommate Billy Brooks walk down chandeliered-hallways to a pre-game meal, then kill time watching television. "The coaches really think we can beat them," said Tinker.

"I don't really show how nervous I'm for a game," said Tinker.

"Take the fight to them," said Switzer in his pre-game speech. "This will be one of the biggest nights in your young life."

Before watching Southern Cal's game against Georgia Tech, Switzer had raved, "They have a super, super team. For us to even have a chance to win we'll have to play a perfect game." But by Game Day, after studying USC game film, and knowing how his own club was rapidly improving, Switzer felt the Trojans were vulnerable, and certainly not as impressive as their vaunted reputation.

"Linemen, they don't slap you, they just muscle you," Switzer shouted as the Oklahoma offensive team watched films of the Southern Cal defense Saturday morning. "You've got to take their butts on — right on the line. We're not going to beat these guys by tricking them," he continued, pacing back and forth, kneading the psyches of his players.

"Men, they haven't played a team that can run the ball like we can. If our defense controls their offense, I'll be disappointed if we don't rush for 400 yards against these people. I'm serious. They have not played anybody who assaults them like we can."

That night in his pre-game talk at the mammoth Coliseum, Switzer was tight-lipped, a calm fury in his eyes as he paced the gold-carpeted locker room floor.

" . . . I don't like John McKay," he told his squad. "He's arrogant, like his football team. They come to the dressing room tonight, they're jiving, snapping their fingers. Hollywood. That's what you're supposed to do out here. We're from Hicksville.

"But remember one thing people: you were recruited to come to Oklahoma to play in games like this. There are 80,000 people out there tonight. All the eyes of the nation are on this ballgame. This is a great challenge, a great opportunity."

Switzer had warned his players, "Don't worry when breaks go against you. If they have success early, there's 60 minutes of football.''

Just as he feared, on the first play from scrimmage, Waymon Clark fumbled the handoff as he went into the line and Southern Cal recovered on the OU 33. Oklahoma's defense held and the Sooners took over on their own 29. Then Davis, after an OU first down, broke into the clear over the right side, only to fumble the ball as he headed upfield. The Trojans recovered on the Sooner 42.

Most teams, playing an opponent like Southern Cal, would have crumbled; the Trojans have that kind of mystique. But again the Oklahoma defense held, forcing a punt. What could have been a 14-0 deficit for the Sooners was still a 0-0 ballgame.

Working from the OU 13, Washington darted 16 yards, Davis cut over left end for 19, and Washington bolted for 17 more straight up the middle. Moments later Davis broke loose for 20 more yards — but the Trojans finally stiffened. Rich Fulcher tried a field goal from the USC 22 but it sailed wide to the right. Soon after, Clyde Powers intercepted a Southern Cal pass, and Oklahoma advanced to the USC 24 before another field goal failed. This time Fulcher's attempt was blocked.

Early in the second quarter, Joe Washington limped off the field with a strained knee. Powers replaced him on the next punt return, only to fumble the ball over to Southern Cal on the Oklahoma 25. Four plays later Pat Haden rifled a touchdown pass to J. K. McKay and the Trojans had a 7-0 halftime edge.

Joe Washington eludes Southern Cal pursuit with an incredible punt return. He took the ball on his own 48, retreated to the 20, then cut back up field and nearly broke loose for a touchdown. His net loss: four yards.

In an unusual departure for Switzer, he gathered up his offense and diagrammed a play while the game was in progress. "We usually drive it down the field and run the same plays," said Tinker.

Tinker slumps on the bench, with a crowd of 84,106 behind him. He caught only one pass for nine yards.

Halftime in the Sooner dressing room was a subdued scene. Most of the players sipped Cokes as they sat in folding chairs or stretched out on the carpet, talking quietly with one another or huddling with coaches. "There was some ass-kicking out there, I'll tell you," said Jimbo Elrod, the defensive end who was taking on players 40 and 50 pounds heavier. Said one Sooner coach, "I've never seen so many big, physical people running around on the same college team."

Switzer told Davis, who had completed only one first half pass (to Owens for 9 yards), "Throw overarm, don't sidearm it." Then he gathered the team around him.

"I think the defense is playing super," Barry said. "If we give the offense the ball, I guarantee you we'll score." He paced for nearly a minute, thinking about the second half. "People, we've got 30 minutes of ball, 30 minutes to play. It all can't go against us like that. It's going our way this half. Thirty minutes of football, cuttin' and slashin'. Let's go!"

The vicious, physical infighting continued in the second half — "it was the worst beating I ever took," Lucious Selmon would later say. The first time the Sooners got possession, they blasted straight at the heart of USC's defense. Grant Burget, his knee in a cast, stood on the sidelines with crutches and marveled as Waymon Clark dove and lunged and clawed his way for every available yard during the drive. "God, he's tough," said Burget.

Finally the Sooners reached the Trojan 2-yard line. Davis faked a handoff to Washington, who leaped high into the right side of the Trojan line. Meanwhile, Davis kept the ball on the sweep left, then cut back into the end zone. It was the first touchdown of the year against the Trojan defense. Fulcher's kick made it 7-7.

That's how the game ended, a frustrating tie, with neither team even threatening to score again.

After watching Tinker diving futilely for badly-thrown passes, a Los Angeles columnist wrote: "Tinker should go to a school where they throw the ball. His talent is being wasted."

Southern Cal's Heisman Trophy candidate, halfback Anthony Davis (above left), could gain only 57 yards against a great Oklahoma defense. He was outrushed by Steve Davis (above right) with 102 yards, Waymon Clark with 126, and Joe Washington with 84.

A glum Barry Switzer paces the sidelines with trainer Ken Rawlinson.

The Sooners were desolated by the tie. They felt they should have won the game — even if it was against the No. 1 ranked team — and the statistics bore them out. A great Sooner defense had held Southern Cal to 102 yards rushing and only 59 passing. The Sooners led in first downs, 18-9, and rushed for 330 yards. But the offense was too lopsided, with Davis completing only one of six passes, the 9-yarder to Tinker.

Switzer allowed his players a few moments for private meditation, then made an effective thrust at their emotions. "I know how you feel, men," he said. "I've got an empty feeling inside. But we're a hell of a football team. A great football team. We whipped them everywhere but on the scoreboard. We can hold our heads high — and they can't. Men, I'm damn proud of you. Damn proud. Hell of a job, men. Super!"

The other coaches, too, were gentle and understanding as they moved about the room, especially to Davis, who slumped on a blue chair, tears in his eyes, blaming himself for the tie. The coaches would pat him on the shoulder, or tousle his hair but Davis wouldn't look up. "It's so disappointing," he mumbled.

"You did the best you could," a radio interviewer consoled.

"I don't think that's true," Davis replied. "You never play as good as you could."

The Sooners flew home immediately after the game, arriving back in Norman about 5:30 A.M. Tinker slept until 1:30, ate lunch at a Dairy Queen, and then joined his teammates for a 3 o'clock meeting. It was time to start thinking about the next game.

"I feel dejected, like everyone else," said Tinker in the post-game locker room. Below, Steve Davis is consoled by Sooner assistant Jerry Pettibone.

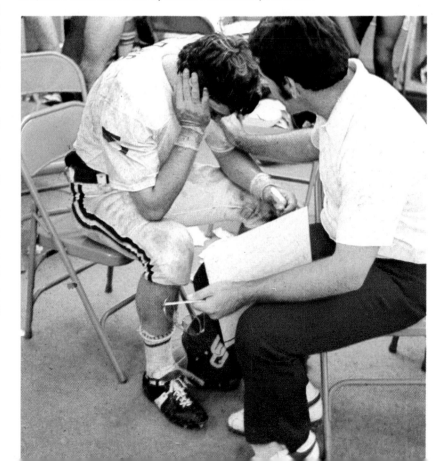

On Wednesday night, the week of the Miami game — and Oklahoma's home opener — Tinker went out and enjoyed his 19th birthday at the Reef. Then it was back to football. He was encouraged by the offensive game plan against Miami, which hopefully would involve him more in the Sooner offense. "Coach Hall says we're going to throw about 15 times against Miami," he noted Thursday.

The Miami game, squeezed between the left over emotions of USC and upcoming thoughts of Texas, posed deeper problems for Switzer than an effective passing attack. On the practice field Friday, he sensed his team was drifting towards an upset and tried to convince them that it would be "a dogfight".

"I wasn't worried about the Southern Cal game at all," he told his players. "But people, I'm worried *sick* about this one." After upsetting Texas, the Hurricanes had beaten Florida State. They were a loose, happy team coached by Pete Elliott, a one-time Sooner assistant.

The night before every game, the OU coaches take the players to a movie. A year earlier they saw a Walt Disney feature, "Run, Cougar, Run," before losing to Colorado — their only loss of the season. That kind of mistake would never be made again. The pre-Miami feature, by contrast, was "The Stone Killer". "It was one of those action-packed ones with all the shooting and blood and all," said Tinker.

Oklahoma scored first. But just as Switzer feared, Miami stormed back to take command, 20-7, at halftime. Then the Sooners finally went to work. Lucious Selmon and Rod Shoate led a ferocious defense that left Miami with a minus-38 yards rushing and only three first downs in the second half. Early in the third quarter, the offense cut the lead to 20-14, and took over at midfield following a punt.

Waymon Clark gained a yard. Galen Hall, who was calling plays from the press box, noticed that Miami's defense was concentrating on the tight end's side, leaving the middle of its defensive backfield vulnerable to the pass.

At the OU 48, Hall called for a post pattern to Owens.

Tinker ran a meticulous pass route. He drove 15 yards at Miami cornerback Ernie Jones, then gave him an outside fake and cut sharply across the field into the open. Davis' pass was almost too strong but Tinker, running at full speed, stretched and caught it on his fingers. He almost stumbled trying to retain his balance but outran Jones to the end zone.

While Tinker was being mobbed by his Oklahoma teammates, Oklahoma kicked the extra point to go ahead, 21-20. A field goal made the final score 24-20.

Davis had rebounded from the Southern Cal game by completing five passes for 123 yards. And Tinker would later reflect, "That touchdown was the first time he gained confidence in his passing." And Davis admitted, "That's the most important pass I've ever completed."

Tinker is in full-flight as he makes the catch which beats Miami, 24-21. Left, he's congratulated by defensive end Gary Baccus.

CHAPTER 4 'GIT IT ON!'

"Regardless of the team records, the excitement is there each year; the game matches state against state, school against school, fraternity against fraternity, oil derrick against oil derrick."
DAN JENKINS,
in "Saturday's America"

Barry Switzer told his players all week, "There's nothing like Oklahoma-Texas. There's nothing like it in college football." And so on Friday, as the chartered bus took the Sooners to the Oklahoma City airport for the flight to Dallas, players and coaches started putting on their game faces.

"Oklahoma-Texas really goes beyond the game," Tinker explained. "There's a

lot of pride involved. Oklahoma and Texas are forever battling over something. It starts in high school with the Oil Bowl, and it just follows all the way up. Dad used to hate those 'dumb Texas drivers,' driving that truck of his."

The Longhorns had rebounded from their loss to Miami to defeat Texas Tech and Wake Forest. They had a powerhouse fullback in Roosevelt Leaks but a defensive tendency which the Sooners hoped to exploit.

"Their safety 'reads' what the center does," said Tinker. "If he blocks for a running play, the safety comes up fast to play for the run. So we worked all week on our halfback pass, where Washington takes the pitch from Davis and fakes a run, while I block on the cornerback. Then I take off downfield and if the safety is suckered in, I should be all alone."

For a receiver with a proven track record on nationally televised games (against Nebraska and Penn State the year before) and one who had caught only four passes in the first three games of the 1973 season, the prospect was downright tantalizing.

At Oklahoma's last practice in Norman on Thursday afternoon, Switzer did his best to bring his players to a properly fanatical frame of mine. All through practice he had the loud speaker blaring a tape of "The Eyes of Texas" and "Boomer Sooner." "It was going continuously through our ears, just driving us crazy," said Tinker. Even Switzer admitted, "I never did like that Texas song. Now I hate it."

Head coach Switzer has his "game face" on as the Sooners ride to the Oklahoma City airport for their flight to Dallas and the showdown with Texas.

OU players wait out those agonizing minutes before kickoff, and then listen to Switzer, who paces back and forth while delivering his pre-game speech.

Nobody goes to school at Oklahoma on the Friday afternoon of Texas Weekend. A majority of the student body is cruising south on I-35, trying to get an early jump on the Friday night revelry in Dallas. "Games have done nothing but ruin great weekends down there," quipped John Keith, the Oklahoma Sports Information Director. Thus the Sooner football team safely encamped at the Sheraton-Fort Worth, 35 miles from the carousing distractions in Dallas.

Friday evening, following their traditional pre-game movie ("Ash Wednesday" with Elizabeth Taylor), the Sooners gathered in the Santa Gertrudis Room of the Sheraton. And while revelers carried on in the bars and restaurants and streets of Dallas, the Oklahoma Sooners sipped hot chocolate and listened to their coach.

"At 12 o'clock tomorrow, kickoff," began Switzer, "you people who have been there know you're going to have the damndest fight you've ever had. ... It comes down to state pride, state universities — who's got the best football team."

Switzer is a persuasive, straight-ahead speaker, who strikes effectively at his team's emotions, and there wasn't a sound in the room as he talked about how Oklahoma could still win the national championship, and about the seniors on the team who had never lost to Texas. He continued to address the team:

"Riding back in the bus there was a lot of talking and jiving about the movie. I was too. I don't sit up there as a coach and worry about those things, turn around and say, 'Knock this crap off, get your minds on the game.' That's not the time to do it. But people, from here on in, I want your minds on the football game and nothing else."

After the meeting the players helped themselves to apples and candy bars and headed back to their rooms. They returned the next morning to have their ankles taped and to review Texas game film for the final time. Again Switzer gave a little talk while three players at a time were taped. The room was silent except for the peeling and ripping of tape by the trainers.

"Last year we tried some new plays that we thought would help our offense," said Switzer. "But every damn time we'd used one of them we'd take a loss, or have it bust, and lose any momentum we had ... People, we don't have but five plays in our offense today. Five football plays that we've run in every football game for the last four years. We're either going to beat their butts or we're going to get our butts whipped on offense by running those plays right at these people."

A police escort spearheaded the Sooner bus through and around a massive traffic jam leading to the Cotton Bowl. At the stadium, Tinker dressed slowly and quietly, concentrating on his pass routes and his blocking assignments. And he listened carefully to Switzer's pre-game talk, which flowed out in stacatto bursts accentuated by long pauses as he paced the floor, arms folded.

"The kicking game will decide the ballgame ... Complete big plays in the passing game ... No mistakes ... Big plays ... Backs gotta fake. You've got to pro-tect the football ... Defense. We've got to gang tackle. Swarm Leaks. Akins, got to intimidate him ... Fifty million people watching you play today ... 75,000 people out there ... A 12 o'clock shoot out. We'll strap the irons on at 12. That's what these Dallas papers like to write. Comments. Sell newpapers ... Poise. Keep your poise.

"Texas is not good enough, people, to take the football and beat us. They've got to have things happen good for them ... There's no bigger ballgame you'll ever play than this one right here. Nothing means more — to the people in the stands, the people on the sidelines.

"...Let me tell you people. You're a great football team. I don't care what the score is. I want you to give a great effort. Let's go!"

After the last pre-game huddle, tense players and coaches take their places on the sidelines.

Tinker scores his second touchdown by running a perfect middle field route, taking the pass in full stride, and racing untouched to the end zone.

Texas received the opening kickoff, was forced to punt, and Oklahoma started from its own 18. Joe Washington zipped 28 yards, and the Sooners ran four more running plays to reach the Texas 40. Already, safety Tommy Keel and cornerback Terry Melancon were rushing up fast and committing themselves to the run.

So the trap was set.

Steve Davis pitched to Washington; who started to sweep right while Tinker faked his block on Melancon. Keel was almost to the line of scrimmage, suckered by the apparent run, when Washington suddenly pulled up and threw a high arching pass to Tinker, who was fleeing down the right sideline, 15 yards in the clear. The closest player, in fact, was fullback Waymon Clark, his arms signaling a touchdown.

"I wasn't thinking about how big a fool I'd look if I dropped the ball on national TV," Tinker said later. "I was just trying to concentrate on the ball, which is hard. I knew there wasn't anybody there, but you get so anxious waiting for the ball to come down, knowing you've got a touchdown if you just catch it."

Trotting back to the bench, Tinker was swarmed over by his teammates — "everybody just seemed to go crazy, banging on my helmet, almost knocking me down" — but the heroics were just beginning.

Early in the second quarter, after Texas had cut the lead to 7-6 with two field goals, Oklahoma had possession on its own 37. This time Tinker ran a post pattern, cutting past Keel. He snared Davis' perfect pass in full stride at the Longhorn 35 and scored untouched.

On a third and 16 situation, Tinker keeps third quarter touchdown drive alive with this leaping, 19-yard reception.

There were 29 seconds left in the half and Oklahoma still led 14-6. The Sooners had possession of the ball on the Texas 47. An obvious passing situation, especially when the Sooners flanked Billy Brooks on the left and Tinker on the right. Yet Davis got protection long enough to heave the ball to Brooks, streaking down the left sideline. Somehow he snatched the ball away from two defenders and sprinted into the end zone. With just three pass completions, Oklahoma had gained 150 yards — and a 21-6 lead.

Despite the margin, Switzer wasn't about to let up on his players. "We got it the easy way," he told them. "We snapped exactly 20 plays the first half. I do not know whether we can take the football and knock their butts out of there and go down the field. That's not the easy way. Texas has proven to me that they can run the football. They have controlled the football. They've had 40 plays on our defense and our defense is tired.

"Let me tell you people," he continued, his voice rising in anger. "To win the ball game you people have got to knock their butts out of there! We've got to control the football! Them damn passes, we were luckier than hell. But we did it, so that's good."

Then Switzer huddled with his offense in front of a blackboard, which carried the exhortation: "Don't Fumble; Don't Crumble!"

"Here's what we're going to do," he said, and he sketched the 71-pitch: the ball would go to Washington and Tinker would fake a pass route, then block down ("crackback") on the linebacker, clearing the way for Washington.

Next, Galen Hall got in front of the blackboard and told his offense, "We'll hit the block pass on them one more time this

game 'cause we're going to hammer and hammer and hammer, and the safety's going to get tired of playing pass. He's going to try to get in the game, and when he does, we'll hit him. And that's easy.

"But men, I'd like to go out there and take the kickoff and hammer at them, take about seven or eight minutes and go score, and now we got them 28-6 and they have to catch up on our defense."

And so Oklahoma went out, took the kickoff, and Davis called three straight running plays to produce a first down. Then the Sooners executed exactly like the X's and O's on the dressing room blackboard. Davis pitched to Washington, Tinker slammed the linebacker to the ground, and Washington burst into the secondary for a 37-yard gain down to the Texas 29.

Three plays later, on a third-down passing situation, Tinker ran a curl pattern and leaped high to catch the ball on the Texas 15. Then Davis, with a key block from Washington, cut over left tackle for the touchdown.

Oklahoma had marched 77 yards in eight plays to tuck the game away — but the rout was just beginning.

The blackboard play springs lose Joe Washington for 37 yards, aided by Tinker's "crack-back" block on unsuspecting linebacker Bill Yeoman — just as diagrammed.

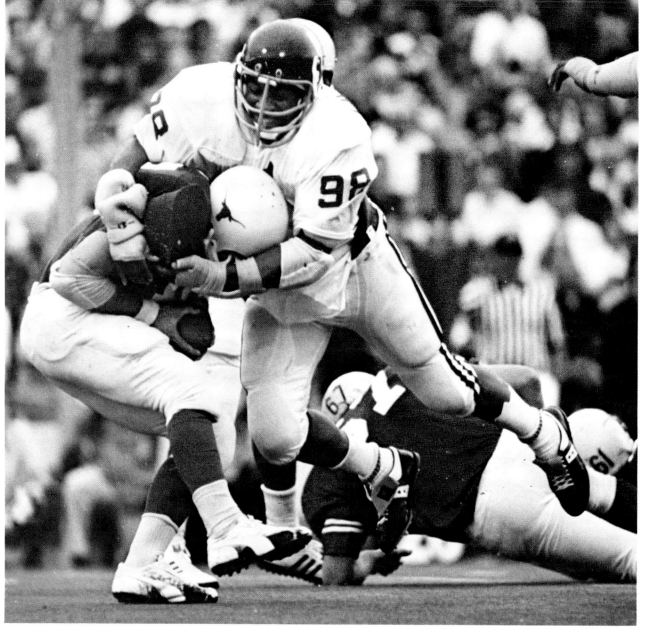

"It was a nightmare out there," said Texas quarterback Marty Akins, wrestled down by Lucious Selmon (above). LeRoy Selmon, recovering from an illness, joined his brothers, Lucious and Dewey, to form the heart of OU's defensive line.

Steve Davis delights in the defensive play — and the score, "I've never been in a more thrilling, emotional game."

Early in the third quarter, a game which had been predicted as a ferocious defensive struggle was suddenly becoming the worst defeat in Darrell Royal's coaching career.

An interception by Clyde Powers led to another touchdown run by Davis, and a fumble recovery by defensive end Mike Struck set up a Fulcher field goal. Oklahoma's good fortune was such that after another interception by Powers, Scott Hill ran for an apparent touchdown — only to fumble the ball when he was tackled at the goal line. But freshman guard Jaime Melendez fell on the ball for the six points, making the score 45-6, with most of the fourth quarter yet to play.

Texas partisans were escaping the Cotton Bowl by the droves while friendly Sooner fanatics waved good-bye and chanted 'We're No. 1!' (In fact, Oklahoma would move up to No. 3 in the national polls behind Ohio State and Alabama). For three years now the Sooners had been able to escape the "poor Okie" taunts by the Longhorns.

Switzer was willing to settle for the 45 points when he sent Joe McReynolds in to quarterback the scrubs from the OU 19 late in the game. Joe had failed to play in the first three varsity games but guided the freshmen to runaway victories over Arkansas and Tulsa. Now he would make his debut as a Sooner, with instructions from Switzer to keep the ball on the ground and run out the clock. Joe didn't throw a pass but he drove the scrubs for a touchdown, running the last 11 yards himself on an end sweep with 1:39 remaining.

The score stood 52-13 and Lucious Selmon sat on the bench, gazing unbelieving at the Cotton Bowl scoreboard. Nearby, Tinker Owens was shouting, "Git it on! Git it on! I'm feelin' GOOD!"

Tinker had missed the school record for passing yardage in a game (with 163) by just 2 yards. He had caught a fourth pass — on a post pattern from the left side — good for 41 yards, breaking free for an instant before one last defender pulled him down at the Texas 21. "Damn, it made me mad that I couldn't shake that guy," Tinker said afterward. "I didn't have any idea what the record was, or that I was close. But I've got the rest of this year and two more years. I'm not worried about breaking it. The way we went today, I think we'll pass a lot more now. Everything turned around.

"Heck, we'll never run the Pro-I at OU. But we've got to pass. If Steve can get it there I should be able to catch it."

Lucious Selmon was named the game's outstanding defensive player by ABC

while Clyde Powers was given a game ball by Switzer. There was also the brilliant play of senior linebacker David Smith, who made 15 tackles, and senior safety Durwood Keeton, who had 17.

Joe Washington, meanwhile, who "gives you a leg and then it's gone," zipped and zagged for 117 yards in 12 carries, to gain over 100 yards for the third game. Steve Davis ran for two touchdowns and completed five of six passes for 185 yards. Tinker himself averaged 40.8 yards a reception.

As Switzer passed Davis on the way to the shower afterwards, he said, "Steve, you're getting better."

"I'm earning my scholarship, coach," Davis beamed.

As the game wore on, coaches and players stop by Tinker's place on the bench for happy handshakes.

Trainer Ken Rawlinson gives Oklahoma's traditional fourth-quarter salute.   "Boomer Sooner" quickly drowned out "Eyes of Texas."

The Oklahoma bench area was just one continuous celebration, as players and coaches embraced and congratulated one another. "Probably the worst injury of the game was coach Hochevar," said trainer Ken Rawlinson. "He wrenched his back on the sidelines. Coach Pettibone was hugging him and holding him up in the air and he hurt his back." In the closing minutes, Switzer instructed his aides to order the players "to show some class, be humble" when talking to the press. He didn't want gloating quotes pinned to bulletin boards providing motivation for the Longhorns next year.

Joe Washington (left) is greeted by his father — who was his high school coach — halfback Bob Berg, and coach Wendell Mosley. The Sooners (above) are a celebrating team well before the gun sounds.

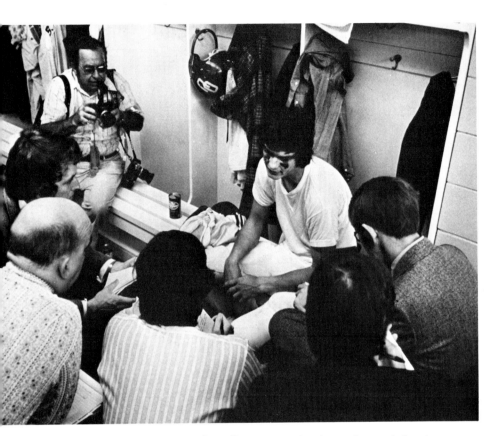

"We had a great game," Tinker tells reporters who clustered around after the game. "We went out and kicked them."

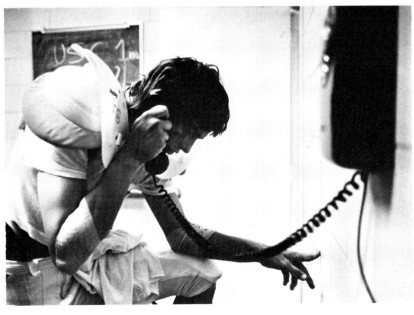

"We're shooting for the No. 1 spot," he tells NBC radio, who got a call through to the OU dressing room. "That's all we want."

Before the press was allowed into the Sooner dressing room, Switzer climbed up on a box in the middle of his cheering players.

"People," he said, "you proved something to me the second half. You played offense and you played defense. Super!

"Now listen up. When we get back I'm going to give a game ball to every senior. And on it is going to be written: 'I played three years at Oklahoma. I never lost to Texas'." The room shook with a roar of approval.

Moments later Tinker was holding court for reporters, recounting his touchdown passes, and trying to explain why he always starred in televised games. "I don't know what the deal is," he said. "I must be a national TV freak."

Back in Norman that night, most of the coaching staff gathered at Switzer's house, where he gleefully carried around a tape recorder that offered "The Eyes of Texas" on request.

"When you play the Wishbone the split receiver is a ghost," said defensive coordinator Larry Lacewell. "You get concentrated on stopping the run and you never realize he's out there until suddenly he comes from nowhere and hurts you. Most of the game, Venus de Milo could play split receiver. Tinker is a Venus de Milo with arms. I've never seen a receiver make so many great catches with such few opportunities."

Meanwhile, the players celebrated at the Pub, where the jukebox blasted out everything from "Boomer Sooner" to "Lord Help Me, Jesus," and tables were drawn together for a free buffet. "Git it on!" shouted Tinker, who was there with Terri. "Git it on!"

Tinker signs a program outside the dressing room. Another girl had him sign her T-shirt.

Randy Hughes and E. N. Simon play Crazy 8's on the flight home while Steve Davis kibitzes.

On the happy way home, Tinker enjoys the scenery on the Oklahoma team charter.

Meanwhile, up in the front cabin, Switzer writes the final score on his napkin and shows it to his coaches before sitting down for the meal with his wife.

"I don't give a damn what happens," he said. "The score will never change."

CHAPTER 5 THE WELL-OILED MACHINE

"This is a rural state, and our football gives John Q. Public something to identify with — something to stick out his chest about and say, 'Boy, I'm a Sooner! I'm part of the Big Red!'"

WADE WALKER
Oklahoma Athletic Director

Just the way the phrase rolls off the tongue — "Oklahoma football" — produces a siren call to blue-chip athletes and brilliant coaches across the Southwest. Feed these ingredients into an athletic program that has money and the facilities, and the result is a quintessential football powerhouse — physically gifted, with an instinct for winning that has become ingrained in the Sooner psyche.

In 1968, for instance, head coach Chuck Fairbanks felt that his outmanned Sooners drew on this spirit when they handed Kansas its only defeat of the regular season.

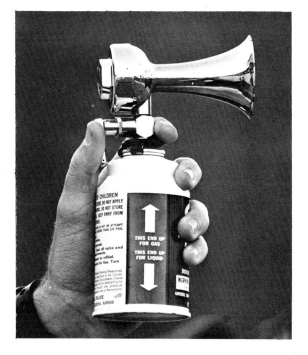

"The Oklahoma teams of the past had quite a lot to do with it," Fairbanks told reporters.

"OU tradition is a big advantage," admitted Tinker Owens, who spent his Saturday afternoons as a youngster listening to the Big Red Network. "Oklahoma players have always been winning football players. That's what I consider myself, and I guess most of the other players feel the same way. When we go out on the field against a team like Baylor, we're thinking, 'There's no way they can beat Oklahoma.' It's just tradition that Oklahoma doesn't lose to teams like that."

There's another reason, too, why the Sooners have been the most successful team in college football over the past 25 years. "We go first class, everything we do," said Tinker. "You can't really gripe about anything. It all makes you feel better than the other team before we even go on the field."

Backdropping this tradition is a meticulous organization. Equipment manager Jack Baer, for example, loves to keep his storeroom shelves neatly stacked and full to the brim. And business manager Ken Farris precedes the team on road trips to insure that logistics are in order. When the 1973 Sooners arrived in Dallas for the Texas game, and the bus wasn't there waiting to take the team to their hotel, Farris stormed, "That's the first time that's happened in 24 years!" And nobody could dispute him.

This careful attention to detail extends down to daily practice sessions. They are planned to the minute and mimeographed off for the coaches. A team manager actually signals the end of each drill with a blast on his air horn.

All practices begin and end with Switzer talking to his team in the middle of the field.

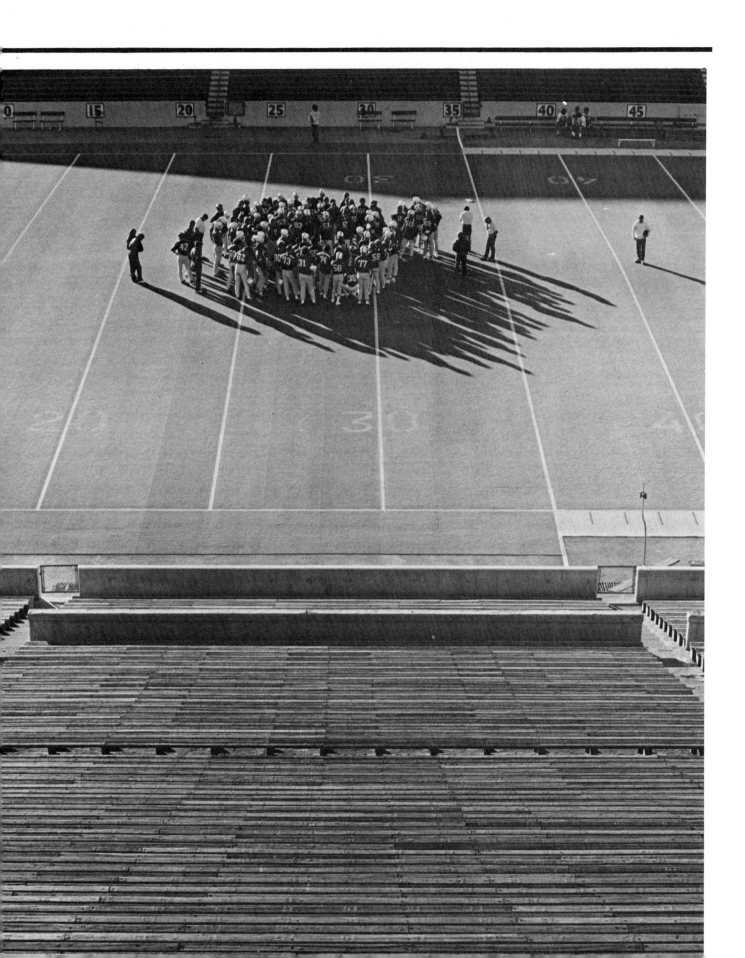

Barry Switzer's ability to relate with his players — "There's nothing they've done that I haven't done" — was one of his obvious strengths as a rookie coach. Thus he was sensitive to what the coaching tower symbolized to his players, with a dictatorial figure running practice from above.

"Fairbanks used to live up there," Tinker recalled. "You always knew that one big eye was on you. You could just feel the heat as he zeroed in."

Switzer preferred to roam the sidelines during practice, mingling with his players while the aides ran the drills. But he found that coaching from the tower gave him an

Switzer unwinds in his coaching tower.

invaluable perspective — especially when his offense and defense were working as complete units.

"You can see the whole defensive scheme, how the secondary is reacting, and the pass coverage," he explained. "Offensively, I can see the play being run, all the blocking schemes, where somebody missed an assignment. You just can't see these things standing on the field."

Still, the tower was badly suited to his metabolism. "I don't stay up there long," he said. "I get too restless. I like to move around. I like the personal contact."

Switzer grew up in Arkansas, captained the Arkansas Razorbacks as a linebacker,

and coached there for six years before joining Oklahoma. A sharp dresser with a handsome, youthful face, he exemplified the new breed college coach: one with fiery intensity and absorption in the game, but laced with humor and an openness toward his players.

"Switzer always has something funny to say during practice," said Tinker. "He doesn't just run our ass all the time. Or in a meeting, you can say something funny and he'll laugh. I think it's good to get a coach like that who doesn't gripe all the time. Switzer jokes around but we know how serious he is. He doesn't ask that much of us — but the discipline is there."

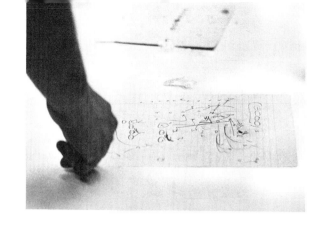

Coaches Don Duncan and Galen Hall.

Running back coach Wendell Mosley.

Offensive line coach Gene Hochevar.

Oklahoma's football staff, which had a coach for nearly every aspect of the game except weather forecasting, would meet every morning during the week at 8:30. They would map out that day's practice schedule, discussing what each coach wanted to accomplish, then review personnel changes (players moving up or down on the depth chart). Later in the season they would begin to evaluate high school and junior college prospects.

At about 10:30 they would break up to individually study film and prepare for the upcoming game. After lunch would come 2 o'clock meetings with their respective players, then practice at 4. Early in the week the coaches usually would return to the office after dinner to pore over more game film.

The same reputation that lures top-quality athletes to Oklahoma also entices the kind of coaches who can develop that talent to its fullest. When Switzer became head coach, he asked Bobby Proctor to become his defensive backfield coach. The 42-year-old Proctor had been at Vanderbilt for six years; his secondary had led the nation in pass defense the previous season, and his friends and ties were in Nashville. Yet he snapped at Switzer's offer.

"It's Oklahoma — what else can I say?" Proctor explained. "Coaches want to get ahead; they dream of going to a place like this."

He had coached at Arkansas, Tennessee, Georgia and Mississippi State. "But Oklahoma," he said at mid-season, "is like moving from hell to heaven. I've never seen athletes anywhere like they have here. I've seen entire conferences that didn't have as many good players as they have on this one team."

Coaching staff gathers for its daily 8:30 a.m. meeting.

As the season moves into November and the shadows lengthen, the weather begins turning cold and sometimes wet. "If you slip and fall, you're wet the rest of practice," Tinker says.

Barry Switzer was like any coach the way he treasured blue-chip athletes. "They're the ones who make the game-winning plays," he said on the eve of the Texas massacre. Switzer's trick, though, was not only to corner more top players than 90 per cent of his rivals, but to design practices which kept this talent happy, healthy and ready to pull off the game-breaker.

"We have intelligent athletes, skilled athletes, people who have proven themselves," Switzer said one day. "Unnecessary work will simply detract from their performance. Tinker Owens doing agility drills for 30 minutes every day after practice isn't going to improve his athletic ability. He's a good athlete to begin with."

"So when you have good players, it's easier to be more relaxed, not as demanding — physically. But demanding mentally. You have to have their complete mental concentration." Thus there were no long scrimmage sessions, and practices ran less than two hours.

"Our practices have a fast tempo," said Galen Hall. "There's very little standing around. To go through one of our workouts you've got to be in pretty good shape." Although the coaches would do their share of shouting, of jumping on players who had goofed up, or who weren't hustling, there was little of the demeaning harrassment that sours football for athletes at other schools.

"We don't have the type of kids where you have to go yell and scream and kick and holler," said Hall.

Switzer poses with the Selmon brothers. "I wish their old man was still producing some more like them," he said.

Eric Hochevar, the coach's son, came to practice one day wearing Tinker's number. He fielded a punt and was carried upfield by one of his blockers.

Prospects Keith Thomas (left) and Horace Ivory watch practice from the tower with Switzer and Pettibone.

Out-ot-town newspapers keep OU coaches in better touch with the prospects they are recruiting.

An automatic machine helps type out recruiting letters.

Oklahoma's football machine was humming smoothly — undefeated after Texas, with a 29-4-2 record over the past three years. But already the pressures were mounting on Jerry Pettibone, the recruiting coordinator, to begin corralling the talent that would keep OU on top in 1974 and beyond.

"As soon as you sign up one group of recruits, you're working on next year," said the gregarious Pettibone, a former Sooner halfback. "It's a never-ending cycle of continually feeding the program with young, quality players. You can't have one bad year of recruiting, or you'll feel it eventually. Maybe not right away but when that class becomes juniors or seniors."

Pettibone's importance at Oklahoma is reflected not only by his office, which compared to Switzer's is almost as large and certainly as plush, but also by Switzer's own admission: "It's hard to out-coach people any more. You have to out-recruit 'em. I'd like to have nine Jerry Pettibone's."

Each Sooner coach except Switzer had a geographic area of responsibility — mostly in Oklahoma and Texas — with Pettibone traveling into every section. They all would watch as many games as possible during the high school season, attend practices, study film, evaluate grades and talk to coaches and teachers about an athlete's attitude and character.

By December, 1973, a secondary list of 500 was pared to 65 prime prospects. These players were then invited to spend a weekend on campus — to meet the players and coaches, tour the facilities and attend a fraternity party. Meanwhile, Pettibone and the coaches started going into homes to meet the parents and continue a selling job that Oklahoma tradition had already begun.

"In our part of the country it's a real honor if your son plays at Oklahoma," said Pettibone. "I've never met a high school recruit whose eyes didn't light up when I told him I was a football coach at Oklahoma."

Of course, this reverence was not always shared by out-of-state athletes. One Sunday afternoon Pettibone brought a heavily-recruited, junior college lineman from California into Switzer's office.

"Coach, before we get started there's a couple of things we ought to get straight," the recruit told Switzer. "I've got to have some threads on my back. I've got to have

Jerry Pettibone's plush outer office has framed reminders of OU's football success.

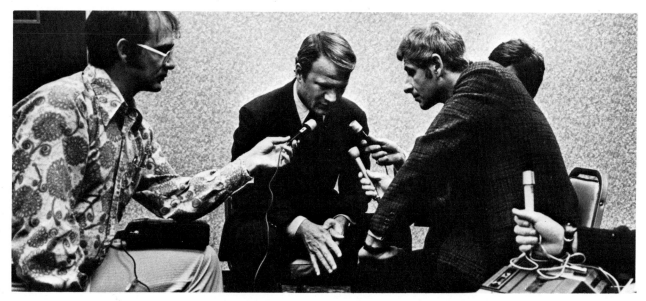

Oklahoma football is promoted not only on Saturday afternoons but whenever Switzer meets with the news media. Above, he is interviewed before his Monday press luncheon.

some wheels beneath my feet. And I've got to have some jingle in my pocket. Then I might think about coming here."

Switzer glared at the recruit, struggling to control his fury. "There's not gonna be any threads on your back," he said slowly. "There's not gonna be any wheels under your feet. And there's not gonna be any jingle in your pocket. If that's what you want, we're not interested."

The recruit shrugged his shoulders and got up to leave. "Well, okay coach. We just saved a lot of time."

"We sure as hell did!" Switzer stormed. The player headed for the door and gave a little wave. "See you around, coach."

In retrospect, that was only a mild irritant, as Oklahoma landed another bumper crop of athletes: Elvis Peacock, the nation's most sought-after running back (6-2, 195 pounds with 9.5 speed); linebackers Joel Estes (6-6, 235) and Dan Mc-Cullough (6-1, 215); Oklahoma tackles Jeff Ward (6-5, 265) and Sam Claphan (6-6, 250); and Norman quarterback Dean Blevins.

A question-and-answer session (above) follows the Switzer luncheon. Every day after practice he briefs Kevin Kuhn and Bill Hancock of the Sports Information Office.

On game days, Norman used car dealer Big Red fields his own team — on his own all-weather field.

To a banker, it's not enough to be the best bank in Norman — or Oklahoma.

Norman even has a new street name by mid-season.

For the fall season, Norman's Adams Chevrolet special orders a fleet of red and white "Sooner Specials."

Pro scouts are daily practice spectators.

Like a South Bend, a Lincoln or a Tuscaloosa, Norman (pop. 52,117) is a college football town. Period. "That's all the people think about is football — and winning," said one citizen. OU coed Stephanie Miller added, "Football is everything; it's just the life here."

On Saturday afternoons when the Sooners are at home, businesses on Campus Corner (the student shopping area) shut down before the kickoff and open back up after the game. "You could rob a store during the game and nobody would bother you because they're all at the game," said one OU official.

The madness that prevails around a winning football team is reflected by the fact that there are as many as 50 small firms producing and selling novelty items from bumper stickers to toilet tissue, all of which are emblazoned with slogans boosting the Big Red. A more beneficial fallout of this mania is an active Touchdown Club, with 1200 members who kick in at least $100 a year. In addition to providing football scholarship aid, the T-Club bought the Tartan turf for Owen Stadium and built a $50,000 weight-lifting room.

There are also 70 members of the Beef Club — who donate a beef or $500 to the athletic dining hall — and 60 members of The Winning Edge, who give $1,000 apiece to the scholarship fund. Other alumni loan out their private planes during the recruiting season. Fueled further by contributions from individuals within Oklahoma's oil industry, the OU athletic department is self-sufficient.

"OU football is really the main thing in Oklahoma," said Tinker. "Everybody's following us and nobody's griping. Hell, they can't gripe about us losing 'cause we don't lose that often, maybe once a year."

Assistant athletic director Leon Cross and Sheriff Bill Porter, a frequent visitor at practice.

Future Sooners are already being recruited.

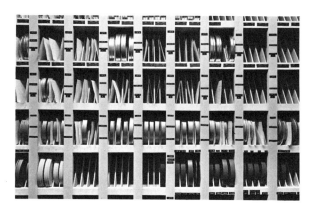

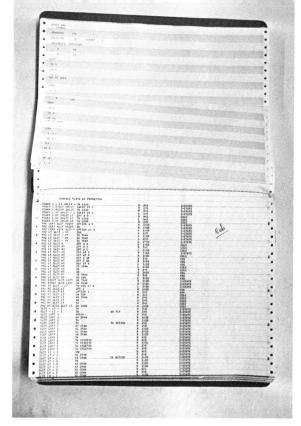

Coaches review Saturday's game film on Sunday morning.

The camera's eye — from movies to Polaroids — was an important adjunct to the Sooner machine.

By Sunday morning, Saturday's game film would already be processed and broken down into offense, defense and kicking game. The coaches would watch the film once for fun — chortling over big plays, and replaying the gems, such as the Washington-Owens pass against Texas. Then they would grade the performance of their respective players on every play, usually with a "plus" or "minus" or "no grade" when nothing happened. Even on running plays Don Duncan would grade his receivers on their hustle, how fast they got off the line, how well they faked their pass routes, how well they blocked. "If you're lined up right and they sweep left, you're expected to get across field and try to block," said Tinker.

Sunday afternoon the players would come over to watch the film. "It's fun, like after a big game," said Tinker, "but most of the guys are dead, they just want to get it over with."

After Sunday, the focus shifted to the upcoming opponent. Every day the players and coaches would study game film of the opponent. The receivers, for instance, would analyze the opponent's pass defense. "We'll look at maybe one film five or six times, watching the same things,

Tinker and fellow receivers study film of an upcoming opponent's pass defense.

trying to see what the defensive backs are going to do," said Tinker.

Meanwhile, a Sooner scout, using game film and his own personal viewing, had fed information into a computer, which gave a readout of the opponent's offensive and defensive "tendencies." This information would be incorporated into the "Game Plan," and drawn upon on Saturday.

During the game itself, an assistant would take Polaroids from the press box a split second after the ball was snapped. "It shows how the other team is lined up defensively, depending on the down and distance," said Galen Hall. "Maybe you'll find something that you hadn't noticed with your eye. Then at halftime you can go down and show your quarterback and the coaches. It's not just a mental picture but something physical that you can look at."

Coaches take a noon break from game films to watch more film — on Sunday's NCAA Highlights on television.

Oklahoma's band rehearses in Owen Stadium with director Thrailkill using Switzer's coaching tower.

As long as football has a halftime, Oklahoma will have a marching band. "We're prejudiced, of course, but we feel the band plays a big role on Game Day," said Gene Thrailkill, director of the "Pride of Oklahoma." "The music has a lot to do with the crowd's response."

"When the band goes to an away game," Thrailkill added, "I think it has a big effect on the team. I know if we didn't show up for a road game like Texas or Nebraska, we'd never hear the end of it."

The band rehearsed every afternoon on a field adjacent to Owen Stadium. Then on Saturday mornings — when the Sooners played at home — they would move into the stadium for a final tune-up.

In fact, the band was like an arm of the football team, receiving $18,000 of its $24,000 budget from the Athletic Department. "We give out scholarships," said Thrailkill, "and we recruit just like anybody else."

Smartly turned out, the "Pride of Oklahoma" has its moment in pre-game and halftime shows.

CHAPTER 6 MEAT ON THE HOOF

"We were moving toward the perfect football mentality. That is, the football fanatic whose total existence and worth is dependent on his football experience."

GARY SHAW
"Meat on the Hoof"

Tinker Owens didn't share Gary Shaw's disenchantment with college football. Playing at Oklahoma, he felt, was an equal trade — a full ride through college in exchange for his football talent. "If I had to pay to go to school, I couldn't," he said flatly. "I'd probably be in junior college now if it wasn't for OU."

He received a typical football scholarship, which covered tuition ($420 a year for 30 units), room and board ($1,080), all books and fees, plus $15 a month for laundry, the same as when Steve was a student. "Heck, I get a check for $15 and the next day I have maybe a dollar left. I can spend more money and not ever know where it goes." In the summer the football department helps line up well-paying jobs through alumni, as is the case at any university that hopes to compete for blue-chip athletes.

In Tinker's view, the toughest commitment of a football scholarship was that he had to go to school at the same time: "People say football players get their grades and stuff but I think it's harder on us during the season. We're putting in a lot of hours with football — meetings, practices and the games — and it's hard to go to all your classes and study all the time. You're just too tired.

"During the season I don't worry too much about my grades. I just make sure I don't flunk out. It's not a real tough school academically, if you go to class and give it the effort."

During this fall semester Tinker had three classes every Monday, Wednesday and Friday beginning at 8:30 A.M. That was downright agony for someone who by inclination preferred to get up to eat breakfast when everyone else was having lunch. When he would struggle out of bed for his philosophy class, breakfast would consist of a candy bar, eaten on the run. He also had accounting, psychology and Theory of Basketball.

"I don't really burn the grades," he admitted, "but I get by and that's more or less what you've got to do." He had 2.80 and 2.15 averages for his two freshman semesters. The second semester an A in Theory of Track was sandbagged by a D in political science and a "straight F" in algebra.

Tinker's diet: from pre-game steak to a "breakfast" candy bar on the way to class.

The day in class begins early, leaves more food than time to eat it at the athletic training table — and includes more tests than Tinker enjoys.

Even if the energy was there, let alone the interest, it took an iron will to study in the OU football dorm. There were constant temptations and diversions. A card game, Crazy 8's, was played mornings, after lunch before practice, and evenings — "You can't live in that dorm unless you learn to play," said Tinker.

At night, if Tinker was indeed in his room trying to study, teammates would invariably drop by and talk him into taking a "study break" at the Pub or the Reef or Orin's pizza.

One Sunday evening a non-football friend of Tinker and Joe McReynolds visited their room, only to find them both poring over books. "They seemed to be quite demoralized," the friend reported. "They said they had to study again the next night, too — but that they would make up for it Tuesday night."

"I don't just kill the books," Tinker admitted later, "but if I have a test I try to know a lot of it. It's hard sometimes. You have a test on Friday but you've been studying film all week, thinking about the game Saturday, and on Thursday night you just don't feel like studying for a damn accounting test. You're thinking about the game."

Counting on professors to help support the football program was risky business. "Some teachers, if you're a football player, they may be lenient between a B and a C," said Tinker. "But others will give you the C. They won't give you the benefit of the doubt."

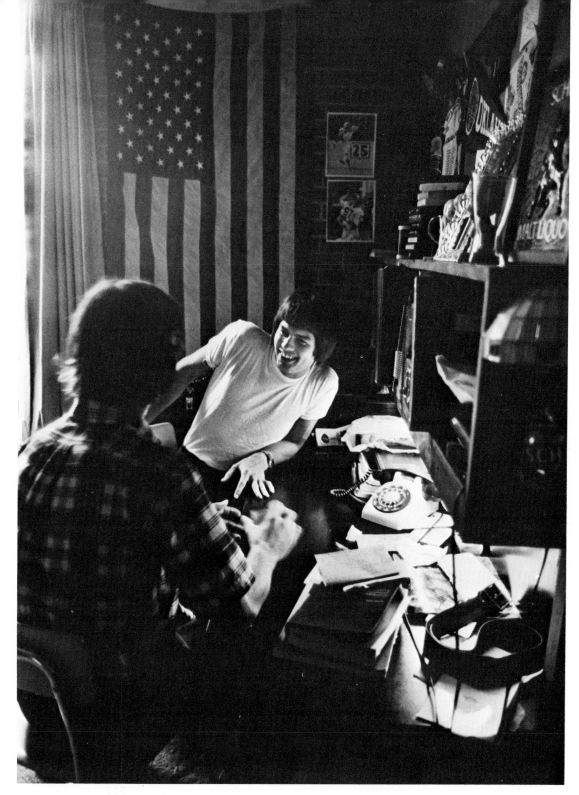

Constant card games of "Crazy 8's" are the rage of the athletic dorm today. But for 35 years, Morris Tenenbaum has guarded the dressing room door — and passed out sticks of chewing gum before practice.

As if the classroom tests weren't enough, the coaches have their own tests before practice.

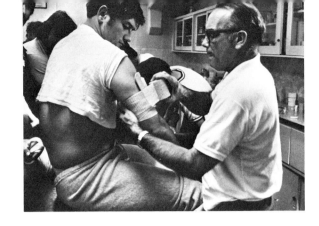

The OU training room had been Ken Rawlinson's bailiwick for 20 years. Like most trainers he tried to joke away what he considered minor or imagined ailments. But when a player was injured he had to come to the training room three times a day for treatment.

Rawlinson was also a "wall decorator," pinning articles to his bulletin board which he felt the players should read. A foe of all drugs, from steroids to pep pills, he put up a newspaper story one morning that was strongly anti-marijuana. Later, John Keith and Barry Switzer walked into the dressing room just before practice.

"Everybody sure is quiet today," said Keith.

"Hell, everybody's in shock. They just read that article," Switzer joked.

Trainer Rawlinson loves to post newspaper clippings on his training room walls.

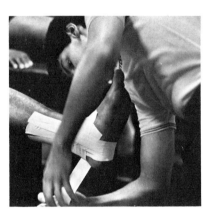

Linebacker Glen Comeaux has his hands, ankles and forehead taped before one practice.

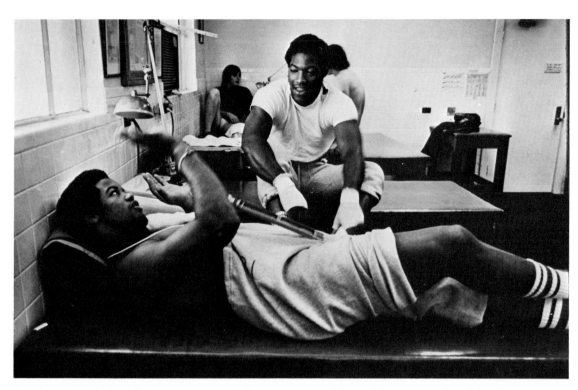

There's a camaraderie and a pensiveness in all dressing rooms. While Rod Shoate can relax while taking a therapy treatment (above), Wayne Hoffman (below) may have to consider if his injury will sideline him on Saturday.

Game Day always began with the team breakfast in a hotel banquet room, usually at 9:30. "People don't say much if you're late," said Tinker, who was guilty several times, "but it's kind of embarrassing. The coaches give you an evil look."

"When I wake up the day of a game," said Tinker, "I feel terrible. I've never felt like eating much. But some of the linemen will eat two steaks, eggs, cereal, milk and orange juice. That's a lot of food to put away before you go out and try to play in the hot sun."

After breakfast the team filed into another room to watch one last reel of game film on the opponent, with the offense on one side and the defense on the other. Two projectors whirled simultaneously and the individual coaches hovered near their players, barking last-minute advice, exhortations and pet phrases.

Larry Lacewell liked to say, "Give a fanatical effort," and Wendell Mosley would urge his backs to "Run with authority," while Gene Hochevar admonished his offensive linemen to "Get up on that damn ball and come off with some damn urgency!"

Tinker has great hands, except when it comes to tying a tie. Then, he turns to his roommate for help.

While a teammate reads the sports page, linebacker Rod Shoate is lost in his thoughts during pre-game breakfast.

An unhungry Switzer watches breakfast.

Coach Hochevar, who "waggles" from the side-lines, reviews signals with the quarterbacks.

Travel uniforms include red blazers — uniformly shedded for the pre-game breakfast.

A victory party at the Pub features everything from fresh shrimp to turkey drumsticks, all combined with loud music and the revelry from the tables.

On college campuses everywhere, Game Day doesn't end with the final gun — it stretches into Saturday night with traditional post-game partying. Most of the Sooners would gather at the Pub or the Reef or the Onion to hash over the game and unwind.

"I'm sure it's this way every place," Tinker observed after the Miami game. "If you win you want to celebrate. If you lose, you're depressed. Either way you've still got pressure on you from the game and you want to either relax and enjoy it, or try to forget it.

Tinker won't touch drugs, not even marijuana. "It would ruin my career if I ever got caught with it," he said. "Besides I don't need it. I don't need any kind of pills or anything to pep me up. I can be pepped up enough just being myself."

Just as in high school, Tinker's life was centered around football, school work and having a good time; uncluttered by involvement in campus activities and organizations. Though a member of Kappa Sigma fraternity (brother Steve also belonged) he only attended their parties.

Though Tinker's lifestyle was somewhat counter to Steve Davis — a licensed Baptist minister, active in the Fellowship of Christian Athletes — they were good friends.

They were dressing one day after practice, and Davis said, "I don't find it odd to be throwing to someone like Tinker. I don't think there's any real difference between Tinker and me — except that I may *think* what he actually does."

He turned to Tinker. "Have I ever preached to you?"

"You've never had a chance," Tinker grinned, quickly pulling on his letterman's jacket and heading out the door.

Tinker and Terri join for the Saturday night celebrations where the afternoon can be relived.
The nights are relived, too, the next morning which are usually quiet ones in the athletic dorm.

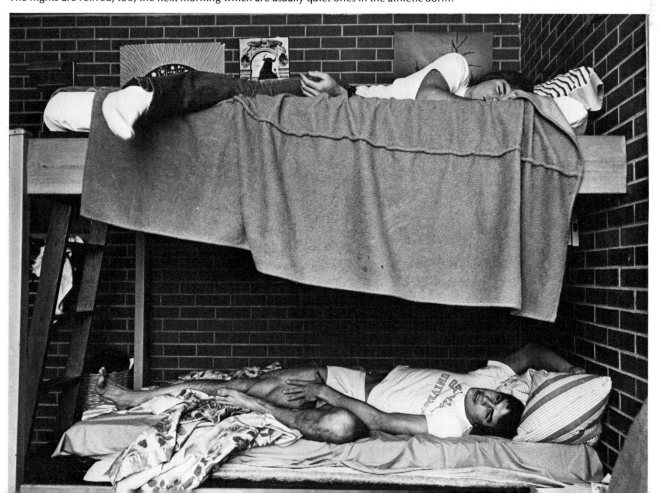

Port Robertson, the school's former wrestling coach, helps shepherd Sooner football players through academia. The "guidance counselor" for all sports since 1954, he's a man the players fear and respect in about equal doses. "You don't want to tangle with Port," said Tinker. "He can take an apple and crush it into apple juice."

Robertson's loftiest goal was to help Student-Athletes map out their academic majors, and get their degrees — even if it took five years. But his job also came down to making sure the players simply attended class. "He really gets on us about that," said Tinker. "He figures if you go to class, the teacher will give you the benefit of the doubt." He was also an influential troubleshooter for those who had problems in school, or off-campus. "If you're in trouble, he'll give you hell. But he'll help you get out," Tinker said.

After football and the victory parties, it's time to check the posted grades and for the words of athletic guidance counselor Port Robertson. Then, back to the books.

CHAPTER 7 CATCH AS CATCH CAN

"Tinker's the best damn receiver in the country, and I just wish we could use him more. But our goal is to win and we win by running the ball."

GALEN HALL
offensive coordinator

The Texas celebration ended phase one of Oklahoma's campaign. For Norman students, 52-13 meant a school holiday on Monday. For Oklahoma recruiters, 52-13 meant an open season on prime Texas schoolboys; Sooner coaches could now move easily about the state and look those Texas fathers right in the eye.

Yet for OU coaches and players, the Monday after Texas meant the start of a whole new season — Big 8 conference play, starting with five games that would lead up to the expected showdown with Nebraska on Thanksgiving weekend.

Out on the practice field Monday, Switzer told his players:

"We can't afford the luxury of savoring the victory over Texas. From here on out we're going to be favored in every football game we play. We have to be mentally mature to handle that. Our fans won't be thinking about Colorado until the kickoff Saturday. All week long they'll be talking about the Texas game. But if we wait until Saturday to start thinking about Colorado, we'll get our butts whipped.

After Switzer's spiel, memory would carry the Sooners up to Saturday's kickoff. A year earlier OU had opened the season with crushing victories of 49-0, 68-3, 52-3 and 27-0 — only to be upset by Colorado, 20-14. That loss probably cost Oklahoma the eventual national championship.

As the team waits to take the field before the Colorado game, tensions run deep and the quiet is shattering.

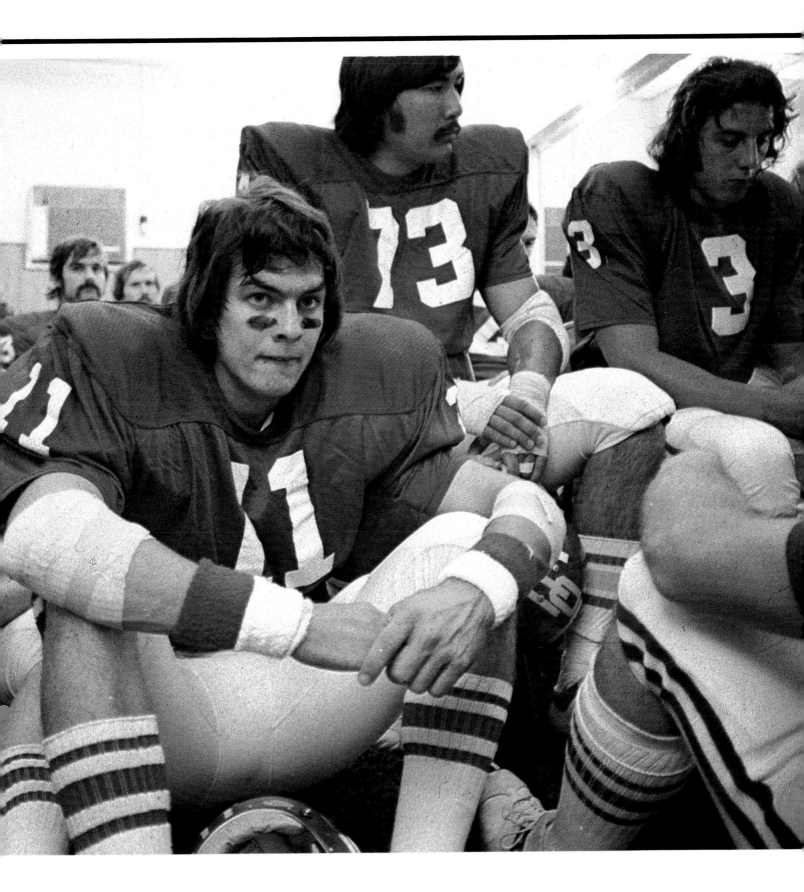

Halftime in the dressing room is often a time of rest, before the coaches reassemble the two units for the second-half instructions.

The day after Oklahoma revenged Colorado, 34-7, Tinker recalled, "I didn't sleep very well at all on Friday night. I had a dream that when we ran out onto the field there was only about 50 people in the stands and it was a rainy day and I kept asking Wayne Hoffman where everyone was. He kept saying 'Don't worry about it, they'll show up.' But they never did."

In real life, though, 61,826 packed Owen Stadium and Tinker felt he had a good day blocking and receiving. He caught two passes for 54 yards, including a tough 47-yard reception that set up Oklahoma's fourth touchdown. Although the Sooner offense reverted to its racehorse running attack, piling up 438 yards while Davis passed for only 93, the Colorado defense always had one eye on Tinker. This left the Buffaloes vulnerable to Sooner trickery.

Colorado was leading 7-0 in the first quarter and Oklahoma had the ball on the Buffalo 37. Noticing the defensive attention on Tinker, and the fact that it was coming up fast when Joe Washington got the pitch, Galen Hall called for a play that had been rehearsed all week. Davis pitched to Washington, who headed right, while Tinker raced downfield — an apparent replay of the Texas option. Only this time Washington lateraled back to Davis, who fired a pass to the wide-open tight end, Hoffman, for a touchdown.

The following Saturday, Oklahoma came into the dressing room with a sloppy 35-7 halftime lead over Kansas State. Receiver Doug Pearson, who was not suited up for the game, whispered, "Coach Switzer's going to really give them hell. But deep down in his heart he knows he's wrong."

100

Oklahoma was just too overpowering. The defense set up five touchdowns during the game and the Wishbone produced 505 yards on the ground. Kansas State coach Vince Gibson (who had philosophized earlier in the season that, "Hard work is worth paying the price for") made more sense after the game. "There isn't a better football team in the country," he said. "If they played Southern Cal now, they'd beat them three or four touchdowns."

Tinker Owens, though, caught only one pass and was growing disenchanted with what his Texas heroics had produced — defenders swarming all over him, "laying back" to prevent his game-breaking deep routes. This was flattery for his receiving skills, but you can't catch flattery.

Oklahoma's success with the running game freed Switzer and Hall to play the percentages — to use the pass as a game-breaker, and to also shift the attention away from Tinker. Against K-State, for example, Joe Washington gained 52 yards on a pass play, and Billy Brooks scored on a 39-yard reverse.

After home games, crowds of fans wait outside the dressing room door, encircling Tinker and Switzer and lining up for Lucious Selmon.

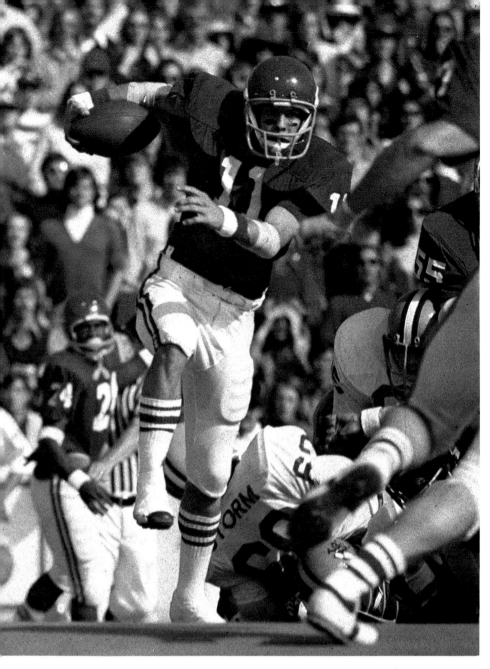

In addition to his pass receiving, Tinker returned kickoffs (above and below against Iowa State). He returned 11 all season for a 17.4 average.

The season moved into November, and Switzer had a premonition that Iowa State — despite its 2-4 record — would give Oklahoma trouble. In his pre-game talk he dropped a score on his players: lowly Southern Methodist 14, Texas 0, at halftime.

"People, that's what scares me," said Switzer. "Teams that sneak up on you and beat you. That's what can happen to you."

Sure enough, Iowa State grabbed a 17-7 second quarter lead, with one touchdown set up by Tinker's fumble of a kickoff. But the great Oklahoma defense stomped Iowa State in the second half — allowing just one first down and 47 total yards — and the Sooners rolled to a 34-17 win.

Tinker was also shut out as a pass receiver for the first time all season. "They only threw one pass my direction," he said glumly. "Then when it was third-and-26 (from the OU 32), they took me out of the game and tried a long pass to Brooks, as if they feel I'm not good enough to run a deep pass pattern." Brooks ran a streak down the left sideline, took the ball away from safety Mark Williams, and jogged untouched into the endzone.

"I was pretty mad after the game," Tinker recalled. "Coach Hall told me, 'I'm sorry we didn't throw more, Tinker,' and I gave him a dirty look.

"I'm not going to say anything. I'll let it ride. I'll just keep my mouth shut and play the way I have been."

Despite his grumblings, Tinker continued to work hard — in practice and during the games, even on running plays when he knew his pass routes were simply a decoy. "I graded out 90 per cent against Iowa State, a real good day blocking and hustling," he noted.

Waymon Clark, a 205-pound junior, busted loose for 172 yards against Colorado and 153 yards against Missouri.

Running sensation Joe Washington breaks into the open. "He should get a game ball every week," said Tinker.

The Sooner Schooner comes thundering down the sidelines after every OU touchdown. Following one runaway victory, assistant coach Jimmy Helms chortled, "There wasn't anything left but popcorn sacks and wagon wheel tracks."

Kerry Jackson, sidelined by Oklahoma's probation, could only watch as Steve Davis took his place and developed into a first-rate quarterback.

Don Duncan, the friendly, knowledge-able receiver coach, suddenly found himself in a dilemma where he really couldn't win — not as long as Oklahoma played with only one wide receiver and one football.

"I don't know if you can keep both players happy in this situation," Duncan admitted in his office one afternoon. The fact that he and Brooks had come up to-gether from Navarro JC put him in an even more delicate situation.

"I know what's going on in Tinker's mind," he said, "when we throw the ball to Billy. 'As long as the team wins that's fine, but I'm not getting enough to catch.' But I have to contend with Billy's thoughts, too. He thinks, 'Hell, I go in there, I catch the football and score touchdowns, why don't I start?' "

Duncan added, "We won't make the decision as to who starts just based on who makes the catch. We have about 75 other plays in the ballgame and if a guy really busts his tail and hustles and does the job, that's a factor too. All you can do is just

For luck, the players tap the sill of the dressing room door.

Against hapless Kansas State, Tinker had to grapple, getting yardage on interference penalties.

try to evaluate them the best you can, and try to have a reason why we do everything. But I'll tell you, I don't feel there are two better receivers anywhere.''

Oklahoma was 3-0 in Big 8 play as it flew into Columbia, Missouri, for what loomed as a traditional trench-fight with the Tigers. Missouri stood 7-1 on the season and was vying for a Cotton Bowl bid against Texas.

The Sooners dressed in the most antiquated locker room on their schedule — a cement-block bunker sunk below the stadium, with six lights hanging from a corrugated roof. "It's like we're back in high school," Tinker grumbled.

Switzer sipped a Pepsi as he paced back and forth in a narrow open area between his players. "I hope we're as ready to play as I think we are," he told them. "I got that feeling inside."

Towards the end of his speech, Switzer paused for nearly a minute, letting the silence seep in as he paced the floor. Finally he said:

"I'll ask you to do one thing when we go on the field today. I haven't asked you to do it before but I think it revs up your motor. I want those people across the way, in black jerseys, and the 68,000 people in the stands, to see Oklahoma frothing at the mouth. I want you to be jumping up and down, acting like a wild man. There's nothing phony about that, people, it's inside every one of us . . . "

At this point the Missouri band started playing the National Anthem. It could be heard in the locker room as Switzer continued, " . . . I want you to slash out and fight and get hit. Go out there, 60 minutes, cut and slash, cuttin' and slashin'. We're Oklahoma — we can always hold our heads up."

The Owens clan meet after games to walk Tinker back to the athletic dorm.

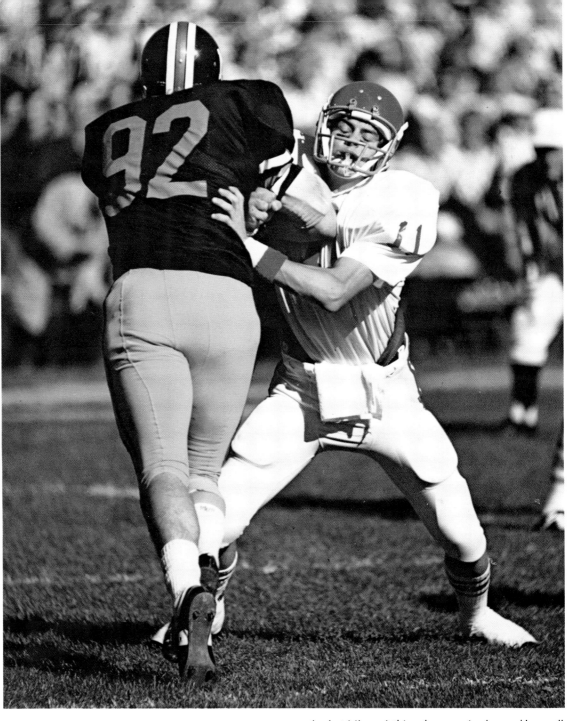

Against Missouri, things began going less and less well.

Tinker bobbles the opening kickoff and is tackled back on the 13.

The Sooners manhandled Missouri, 31-3, playing with the intensity Switzer sought in the dressing room. The defense allowed just six first downs, 44 yards rushing and 64 yards passing. And the offense produced big plays, including a spectacular 80-yard punt return and a 41-yard touchdown run by Washington.

The key play of the game, though, was a 63-yard TD pass play from Davis to Billy Brooks. Brooks ran a short curl pattern, caught the ball, spun free and then outsprinted the entire Missouri secondary. "That was pure speed," raved Switzer, who ran down the sidelines to congratulate Brooks.

Tinker, meanwhile, caught his usual quota — one pass for 12 yards — as Davis could complete only three of eight. Afterward, dressing quickly, there was no delight in Tinker's eyes. "Right before the game, coach Switzer told me, 'I'm going to alternate Brooks more with you today, because he's down. I'm going to do it for his sake.'"

Tinker managed a small grin. "Maybe I should go to Barry and tell him that now *I'm* down."

Tinker had never found himself in that situation before. He had been a high school hero, a varsity star as an OU freshman, and enjoyed early-season success as a sophomore — only to find himself catching fewer passes and splitting time with an equally-gifted rival. Football was Tinker's life and he over-reacted when the coaches began tampering with that involvement. He really couldn't understand the juggling of egos — and talent — that was necessary to keep a team like Oklahoma winning.

Distraught brother Jimbo met Tinker after the game and shed a few tears for Tinker's low point of the season.

By halftime, an angered Switzer rips into his players in the tiny Missouri dressing room. He was unhappy over their poor coverage of punts and kickoffs.

But back on the field, Switzer ran almost to the end zone to hug Joe Washington on his second touchdown that assured the victory.

"Tinker's the best damn receiver in the country," said Galen Hall that night, "and I just wish we could use him more. But our goal is to win and we win by running the ball. That's what this team does best."

Through it all, however, Tinker and Brooks remained friends, taking their frustrations out on the coaches. "I'm not around Billy that much, except on the road," said Tinker. "We get along all the time, really. But we don't talk about the situation. It's not brought up."

Kansas came down to friendly Owen Field with a Heisman Trophy contender — quarterback David Jaynes — and upset hopes, only to be crushed, 48-20. Midway through the second quarter, in fact, the Sooners already had a 41-6 lead and Switzer dipped down to the end of his bench to prevent an embarrassment.

"Scores like that aren't healthy for college football," he said, "but we played 72 people in the game, the most an Oklahoma team has ever used."

All season long the third and fourth string Sooner scrubs — known as the "termites" — would serve as fodder during practice. They ran the plays of each upcoming opponent against the first team defense. Jeff Mabry was the regular "termite" quarterback and his backfield pals dubbed their unit "The Four Horsemen". Finally against Kansas, they were getting their chance to play.

Switzer huddled with Mabry on the sidelines. "Now what plays do you know?" the coach asked.

Mabry hesitated. "Coach, I think we could really do best against them by running *their* plays," he said honestly.

"No," said Switzer, "that would be humiliating. You've got to run our plays." So he gathered the "termites" around him and — lacking sandlot dirt — reviewed several plays by drawing his finger across the artificial turf.

Mabry trotted into the game, and drove the "termites" into scoring position. But then he tried a pass. Kansas intercepted and returned it 92 yards for a touchdown.

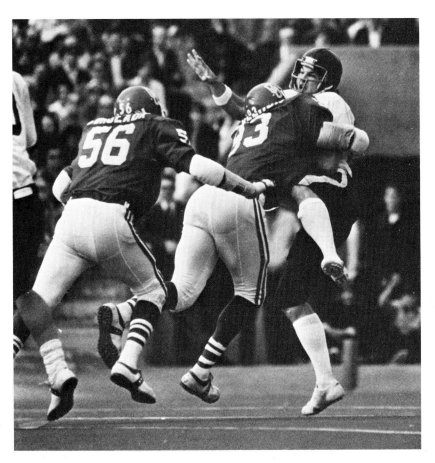

LeRoy Selmon leads the assault on Kansas quarterback David Jaynes. Said OU tackle John Roush: "Jaynes was like a pinball machine, he got knocked around so much I thought his arm was shaking when he tried to throw."

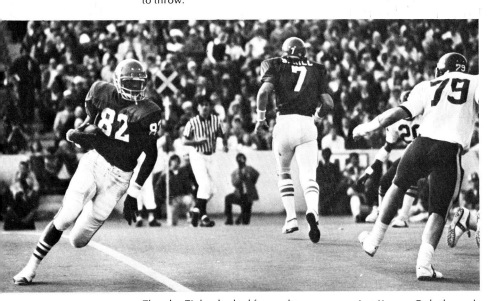

The play Tinker looked forward to was run against Kansas. Only the end-around reverse features Billy Brooks taking the ball from Scott Hill.

It was a school record and within two yards of a national collegiate record when sophomore Tony DiRienzo kicked a 60-yard field goal against Kansas — despite the misspelling of his uniform. Terri and Tinker ate out, somewhat glumly, in a Norman restaurant that night.

CHAPTER 8 THE SHOWDOWN

"Tinker is such an exciting damn player. He's like a show business star. He really knows when that camera is on."

CHRIS SCHENKEL
ABC Sportscaster

Oklahoma-Nebraska, in recent years, had become the traditional Thanksgiving Day offering on ABC. That tradition was now moved to Friday — at ABC's cajoling — so that the network could deliver a three-day package featuring seven of the top eight teams in the country.

Ranked No. 3, Oklahoma still had a shot at the national championship, since No. 2 Ohio State would play undefeated Michigan, and No. 1 Alabama was up against unbeaten Louisiana State. But the Sooners' immediate goal was the Big 8

championship, which they could win outright by beating Nebraska.

Tinker Owens, of course, was charged up about his own individual prospects against the Cornhuskers.

"Heck, I know I'll have a good game — it's on national TV," he grinned. In his three previous appearances, against Nebraska, Penn State and Texas, he had caught 14 passes for 403 yards and three touchdowns — an entire season's work for some receivers. Yet, because of Oklahoma's probation, this would be Tinker's last game on television until he was a senior — "and the only way we'll appear then is to go to a bowl game."

Tinker not only had ABC in his game plan, but he would be working against cornerback Zaven Yaralian, whom he had victimized a year earlier. "I'll have a good game if they give me a chance," he said earnestly.

When Switzer learned the extent of Tinker's disenchantment — before the Kansas game — he was perturbed. "For Chrissakes, why is he down?" Switzer steamed. "Is he down like a halfback who's not getting a chance to carry the ball? Okay. But if we don't give Brooks a chance, he'll leave. We'll lose him in December to another school because he feels he can contribute something.

"Next year no other team in America will have two split-ends as good as Tinker Owens and Billy Brooks. Both first round draft picks. Sure Brooks is more gifted physically — but hell, Tinker's a better receiver. He runs better patterns, he has better hands, and better concentration. So why is he down?"

Tinker was among the players recorded the day before the Nebraska-Oklahoma game, who opened the national telecast Friday afternoon.

Despite what some sports history books might imply, Oklahoma football wasn't invented by Bud Wilkinson, the John Wooden of college football between 1947 and 1963.

One of Wilkinson's predecessors, for example, was Bennie Owen, who as early as 1914 was pioneering wide-open football. Since Owen also had to fill out his schedule in those years with teacher colleges, his Sooners pillaged such schools as Kingfisher (179-0, 157-0 and 104-0), Alva Normal (102-0, 101-0), Shawnee Normal (107-0) and Weatherford Normal (140-0).

Still, it was Wilkinson who brought Oklahoma to national prominence. Dour and conservative as he was personally, Wilkinson produced exciting teams that had slashing speed and aggressive, gang-tackling defenses. Beautifully well-conditioned and self-disciplined, the Sooners compiled record winning streaks of 31 and 47 games. Along the way they won three national championships and 13 consecutive conference titles, leading critics to dub the Big 8, "Oklahoma and the Seven Dwarfs". Finally, though, young coaches like Bob Devaney at Nebraska, Dan Devine at Missouri and Eddie Crowder at Colorado helped build the Big 8 into the strongest top-to-bottom conference in the country.

Another characteristic of Oklahoma football has been the unusual number of famous brother acts. Steve and Tinker Owens were hardly the first. The four Johnson brothers, who were part-Chickasaw Indian, all quarterbacked Sooner teams between 1912 and 1925. In that same era were "The Terrible Hotts" — Oliver, Willis and Sabert, a one-eyed, 162-pound defensive tackle. After World War II came the Burris brothers — Buddy and Kurt (both All-American linemen) and Bob, a fullback — plus All-American guard Plato Andros and his brother Dee, the longtime coach at Oregon.

Yet the most remarkable group of all would have to be the Selmons — Lucious, LeRoy and Dewey — who grew up on a farm outside Eufala (population 2,500) in eastern Oklahoma. They marked the first time that three brothers had ever been in the OU starting lineup at the same time. "The most unique thing about the Selmons is their ability — not their name," said Switzer. "They would be a heckuva line if they were 740 pounds of Smith, Brown and Jones."

Casual and unaffected as he might have seemed, Tinker Owens was aware of who he was. He enjoyed the notoriety that football brought him on campus where the football player was still a hero: "If you're going good and you walk by people on campus, you can hear them whisper, 'There's Tinker Owens.' Guys I don't even know come up to me at the Reef and want to talk football. That's the kind of treatment you get around here, as far as the students and all, 'cause they're following and cheering everything that goes on."

This recognition pursued Tinker following every home game, when young Sooner fans, game programs and pencils in hand, swarmed about him like pass defenders. These youngsters could relate to Tinker more than any other Sooner player: he was hardly much bigger than they were, he was white, and he had that youthful, folk-hero look.

After his freshman year, Tinker had appeared at several sports banquets around Norman and Miami. "I don't like to speak in front of people real well," he admitted. "Sometimes I can get up there and talk all right but other times I get shaky and grumble out words. It's hard to think of something to talk about. I mean what do you talk about except for football?"

That had always been Tinker's life — football, and sports. Brothers Steve, Larry and Dale were all student body presidents in high school, and active in other organizations. "But Tinker," said Olen Owens, "never wanted any of that stuff, the student council or responsibility like that. He just went for that ballfield."

Nor was Tinker really thinking beyond his football career. "They say you have to like something in college, as far as classwork," he said, "but I haven't found anything that I really enjoy doing. Playing pro football — that's what I've always wanted to do. That's really been the main goal of my life."

Another aspect of Tinker's appeal was the fan mail that trickled in (six or eight letters a week) during the season, mostly from midwest youngsters seeking autographs and pictures.

The week of the Nebraska game, however, Tinker opened an innocent-looking fan letter. Inside were three pictures of a nude girl wearing only a Michigan T-shirt. Her note read, "My heart belongs to Michigan but my (deleted) belongs to OU ... I hope these pictures will inspire you against Nebraska."

When Tinker showed the pictures to quarterback Steve Davis, the Baptist minister, Davis shook his head in dismay.

"The only thing I get in the mail," he said, "is Bible passages."

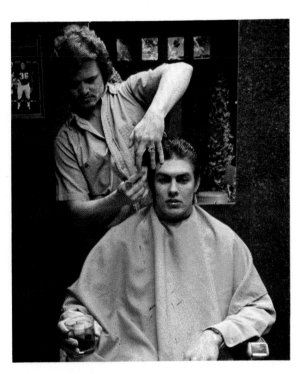

For the weekend, Tinker has his hair cut at Sonny's, where brother Steve was also shorn.

On the day before the game, Switzer visits with Bob Devaney, now the Nebraska athletic director, who built the Cornhuskers into a national power in the 1960's.

Tinker joins brother Larry and his wife for Thanksgiving dinner (top) while most of the team feasts in the athletic dining hall.

While most of the players ate Thanksgiving dinner in the athletic dining hall, Tinker joined brother Larry and his wife Debbee, who lived in Norman. Larry, two years older than Tinker, was a promising athlete himself until sidelined with a bone disease in high school.

Thursday night's team meeting lasted barely five minutes. "Games like Nebraska and Texas take care of themselves," Switzer explained later. "It's the other ones in between that worry the hell out of you, the ones where you're favored and the kids know it. That's when you have to challenge them because they wear the Big Red uniform."

This was another of Switzer's gifts — an ability to lift his team to an emotional high, moments before kickoff. Not with bombast or invective, but direct, old-fashioned appeals to his players' pride, their anger or frustrations against those who had placed OU on probation.

"He never let us feel sorry for ourselves," Tinker said. "He's turned all the bad things into good things. We're a young team and we get emotional over stuff like that. He has us thinking, "We're going to whip their damn ass! We're going to show 'em!""

Switzer would think about his pre-game speech all week but leave it swirling in his head so that his words would come tumbling out spontaneously, 10 minutes before kickoff.

"The game is all that's in your mind," said Tinker. "But Switzer really builds the tension. He'll start saying something, using that fire talk, and everybody is sitting there listening, really tense. Then he says, "Let's go out and get them!" Even someone like Joe McReynolds, the third team quarterback, would get swept up. "Switzer really gets you excited," said Joe. "He makes you want to go out and hit people!"

Not even a shoelace is out of line when OU uniforms are laid out on Game Day.

Before the game, Barry Switzer briefs Bud Wilkinson, now an ABC commentator.

Sooners arrive from their hotel.

Friday's clash between Oklahoma and Nebraska was a physical brawl from the opening kickoff. "That was the most vicious hitting I've ever seen," said OU safety Randy Hughes, in the refuge of the postgame locker room.

Oklahoma gained a 14-0 halftime lead on touchdown runs by Waymon Clark and Steve Davis, and a stunning defense that held Nebraska to just three first downs and 67 total yards. The Sooners played so well, in fact, that Switzer's main worry at halftime was how to sustain their intensity. He simply reminded them that one year earlier Nebraska had led in the second half 14-0, only to lose, 17-14.

Then he told his team: "All right, people, let me tell you what's happening. You have just played the finest defensive half any college team's ever played. Now you have a chance to really do something — to get it up and play like that in the second half and show 50 million people all over this country how a really great team plays."

Once again he drew on Oklahoma's dilemma — this time the upcoming television ban — to provide the clincher. "Let's go out there, and give 'em something to remember for the next two years!" he shouted.

Normally high-strung and restless before a game, Switzer takes a snooze in the coaches dressing room.

Owens and Nebraska defender Zaven Yaralian collide near midfield while going for a pass. Tinker later made a great diving catch near the sideline only to sail out of bounds before his feet came down. Waymon Clark (below) is flagrantly face-masked but no penalty was called.

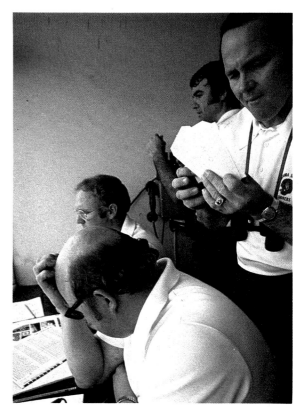

Galen Hall (right, with headsets) and Terri Kinkead (below) typified the unraveling of emotions in the first half. Hall had spent the week developing his offensive game plan, and listed the plays he felt would work against the Nebraska defense. Working from this list, and improvising as Nebraska's strategy emerged, Hall would call the plays and Switzer would relay them to Davis.

Late in the first quarter, leading 7-0 and faced with a third-and-one situation on Nebraska's 47, Hall called for a quarterback sneak. "We just wanted the first down," he admitted. But when Davis bolted to a touchdown, the OU press box coaches went wild.

Tinker's fiancée, meanwhile, watched from the stands. Terri wasn't a cheerleader in high school. "But I get emotional anytime something happens," she said. During the season she drove down from Miami for all six OU games.

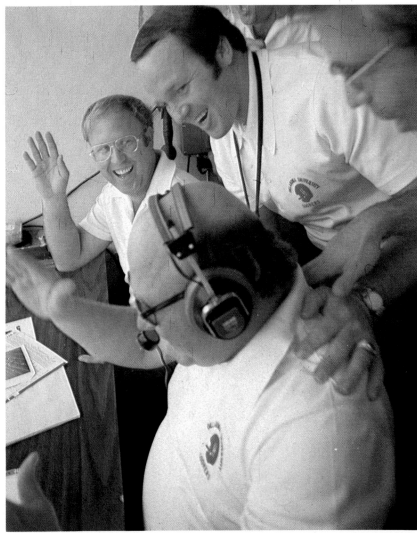

Galen Hall is congratulated by Jimmy Helms, right, and Don Duncan following Davis' TD run.

Hands — and glasses — are held high by exuberant Sooner fans as Oklahoma scores two more second-half touchdowns to overpower Nebraska, 27-0. A sellout crowd of 61,826 jammed Owen Stadium.

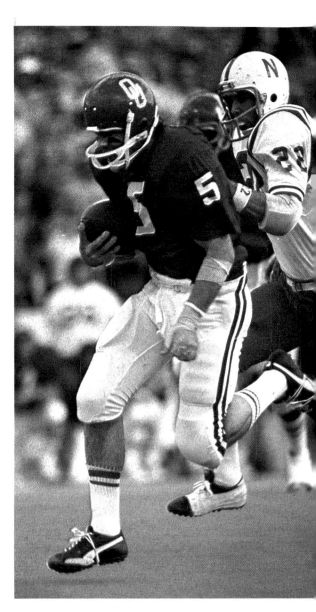

An effective Wishbone attack is dependent on a tough, fast quarterback who can run the ball. Somebody like Steve Davis. He scored three times against Nebraska — from the 1-yard line (above left), from the 47 (above right), and from the eight, after a long pass to Owens.

Although three Sooner touchdowns came on short runs, the real damage was inflicted by OU's big-play capabilities — Joe Washington's 34-yard dash down to the Nebraska six, Davis' 47-yard keeper, and an interception at Nebraska's 26 helped push the score to 21-0 late in the third quarter.

Nebraska, which had entered the game with the nation's best pass defense, allowed just three completions. Despite Tinker's pre-game optimism — and the ABC cameras — he caught only one pass, a 41-yarder that set up OU's final touchdown with three minutes to play.

Tinker ran a deep pattern, faked inside, cut outside, and then cut back into the middle of the field. He took the pass in stride, over his shoulder, but was tackled immediately on the Nebraska eight.

"That's about as well executed as a play could be," commented Bud Wilkinson, who felt that Tinker had the best reflexes for catching passes that he had ever seen.

Savoring the dismantling of Nebraska are Davis and John Roush, a tackle on OU's overpowering offensive line.

Tinker catches this pass (left) but is out of bounds. Later he is greeted by receiving rival Billy Brooks after hauling in a 41-yard bomb from Davis.

Lucious, Dewey and LeRoy Selmon shut off Nebraska's running attack.

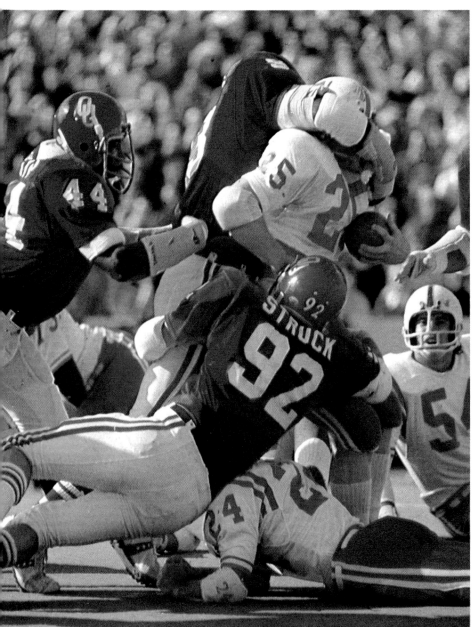

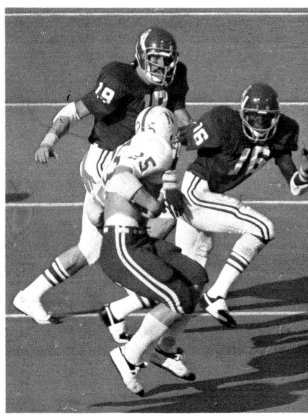

Nebraska quarterback David Humm is sacked by a ferocious defense. He completed only eight of 20 passes for 77 yards.

In the backfield, Randy Hughes and Tony Peters chased down Tony Davis.

Oklahoma's defense — against a team that was averaging 28 points a game — was savage and spectacular. Not only was Nebraska unable to advance past the 50 yard line, it was shut out for the first time in five years. "I would take this defense and go fight Russia," boasted OU defensive coordinator Larry Lacewell.

LeRoy Selmon intimidates Steve Runty.

Tinker, a defensive back in high school, tackles Tom Rudd after an interception. "I tried to hurt him but it didn't even phase him," said Tinker.

Escaping from the field on one shoe, tailback Tony Davis symbolizes the punishment dealt out by Oklahoma's defense. Nebraska's top runner gained only 41 yards.

A "dad-gum happy" Switzer is carried off the field by his assistant coaches, while a Nebraska loyalist wonders when the next bus leaves for Lincoln.

Switzer praises his Sooners and awards a $26 game ball to every player. Then he leads his team in private meditation.

Fleeting images raced through Switzer's mind as he was carried off the field. "The crowd, the excitement, the faces, the mass of red and white," he said. "And just the thrill — the shock almost — of winning the way we did, and knowing the entire nation had a chance to see the complete domination of Nebraska." Yet one thing lodged in his memory. "It was all the assistant coaches carrying me off instead of the players," he said, smiling. "I guess because we were on national TV and they wanted to be in the picture."

Once inside the Sooner dressing room, Switzer was as emotional as his celebrating players, laughing and shouting as tears rolled down his face. But finally he got his team quieted down.

"We're champions!" he bellowed. "We're Big 8 champions!" and the Sooners roared. "I want to tell you — there's no need to tell — how happy we are." He went around the room, singling out the seniors (nine starters would be lost) and the players would cheer each name.

Then he addressed the team again: "You're great! Super! Every one of you. That's a great way to go out, people. They didn't think we could do it. But we did." There was more cheering, and Switzer grinned and said, "People, it's OU 2, Cotton Bowl 0!"

(Nebraska had already accepted the bid to play Texas, which led Terry Webb to quip, "I guess we're the Cotton Bowl champs by about 79-13.")

When the Sooners were again calmed down, Switzer concluded: "Let me tell you, I'm going to do this. Today we give everybody on the varsity a game ball. You're Big 8 champions — every one of you!"

Afterwards, Switzer told reporters: "The nation had an opportunity to see the

Puffing on a victory cigar, Switzer celebrates at home with OU coaches and friends like Bobby Bell, left, his "fishing coach."

finest defensive team in the country. I've never seen a football team play as physical a game on defense." He called junior linebacker Rod Shoate "the best player in the country at his position" and praised Joe Washington: "I haven't seen anyone this year — in a game, on film or on television — who can do the things he can do with a football under his arm."

Steve Davis, meanwhile, was by his locker, savoring the game, the season, and the way he had straight-armed his skeptics. "I don't know why people didn't think more of us before the season started," he said. "They just looked at the statistics and not our hearts. They must have forgotten that we're Oklahoma and we're used to winning."

Tinker Owens, too, was pleased. "I can't believe it," he said. "I figured we'd beat them but I didn't think we'd *punish* them."

Tinker helps himself to more home-cooking while Olen Owens commands his usual post before the living room television set.

After the game, Tinker and Terri drove straight to Stillwater, where Miami High was competing in the state football playoffs. Jimbo played the entire game as a wingback and safety and intercepted a pass which killed a late scoring threat. The game ended in a 7-7 tie, but Miami advanced by having more first downs.

"I think we're going to see a good football player," said Olen Owens the next morning. "Jimbo runs the same way Tinker does, he has the same moves and he has great hands." Jimbo, at 5-11, 150 pounds, was even smaller than Tinker, but he would be accepted at Oklahoma in the spring.

Saturday afternoon Cherry Owens fixed Tinker his second Thanksgiving dinner and then they watched Ohio State escape with a 10-10 tie against Michigan, and the No. 2 ranking ahead of Oklahoma. Tinker's own receiving problems, though, were put more in perspective when Ohio State failed to throw a pass until the last minute of play.

Through all the football fanfare — the heroics, the recruiters, the family noteriety — Olen and Cherry Owens had remained unchanged: modest, frugal parents who had no use for expensive habits or fancy egoes. "They're just very common, very real people," said Steve, who remembered how Olen had called from a truck-stop pay phone to see if his son had won the Heisman Trophy.

Although there were now 12 grandchildren (10 of them in Miami), Tinker could sense that an inevitable change was coming for his parents. "Jimbo is the last one living at home," he said, "and now they know that I'll be getting married. The next couple of years will be really tough on them. All of us kids have been the only thing they've ever had."

Tinker and Jimbo watch in frustration as Michigan misses two last-minute field goals against No. 2 ranked Ohio State. The 10-10 tie ended OU's last real hope for a national championship.

When Oklahoma was routing Big 8 opponents back in the 1950's with scores like 66-0, 67-14 and 65-0, Sooner fanatics just couldn't get enough.

One Saturday, after Oklahoma had demolished Kansas State, 34-0, a Sooner fan called the sports desk of the Daily Oklahoman in Oklahoma City. He asked Jay Simon for the OU score and Simon told him, 34-0.

"What!" the called exclaimed. "Only 34 points?!"

Simon hung up the phone and said out loud, to no one in particular, "How much rice can a Chinaman eat?"

Ever since, the over-zealous Sooner rooters have been known as the Chinamen. They form a network of "correspondents" and "critics" who keep OU football coaches abreast of grassroots opinion — the kind that might not be appearing in Oklahoma's family newspapers, which give the Sooners extensive statewide coverage.

"They're crazy about football, and they love you when you're winning," said sports publicist John Keith. "But drop a couple of games and they start writing letters. They wanted to fire Fairbanks when he was 6-4 and 7-4. Then he went 11-1 and they loved him."

During that troubled stretch, when OU was converting to the Wishbone and losing to teams like Kansas State, the Chinamen dispatched scathing letters to Fairbanks and his assistants.

As the offensive coordinator and the one who convinced Fairbanks to adopt the Wishbone, Switzer saved every letter. Then in 1971, on the eve of the classic with Nebraska when the Sooners were 10-0, he wrote every person back.

"Win or lose, we're going down to the Sugar Bowl," he told them. "Hope to see you there."

OU DEFENSE RULES THE WORLD

Sooners Slug Huskers, 27-0, To Win Big 8

By Frank Boggs
Staff Writer

Sneaky Davis Was Shocked He Got Away

By Volney Meece
Staff Writer

The Daily Oklahoman
Sports
Sat., Nov. 24, 1973   21

Devaney, Royal, Wilkinson Selmonized by Defense, Too

Playback

Bob Hurt

Putnam Squeaks; West, Moore Ousted—Next Page

OU quarterback Steve Davis broke Nebraska's back on this play, cutting through the right side of the line and finding 47 yards worth of daylight for a second quarter touchdown and a 14-0 Sooner lead.

TV-Radio Log

Sooners Show Nebraska the 'Iron Curtain'

Tulsa Tribune
SPORTS
SAT., NOV. 24, 1973
PAGE SIX A

CLEARING THE AIR
Bob Hartzell

Scots Boot Big One

By Bill Shanks

OU'S LUCIOUS SELMON PUTS PRESSURE ON HUSKER QUARTERBACK DAVID HUMM

SOONERS STEVE DAVIS ELUDES ZAVEN YARALIAN (17) FOR TD

Tyson Top Card Rookie

Disappointed Huskers Admit Total Defeat

By Bill Harper
Assistant Sports Editor

K-State Whips Yugoslavians

Kodes Upset In Aussie Meet

How They Scored

HUSKERS TONY DAVIS SEEMS ABOUT TO BREAK AWAY, BUT GARY BACCUS HAS HIM AT ANKLE AS DEWEY SELMON CLOSES IN

Make No Mistake, Offense Was Great

After That First Play, Sooners Were Perfect

By Hank Inman
Staff Writer

SPORTS ...of the TIMES
Sat., Nov. 24, 1973   9

Switzer Calls It 'Finest I've Ever Seen'

...and Defense Simply the Ultimate

Frank Boggs

Joe Washington does a lot of fancy stepping in a lot of fancy places, but this one probably didn't suit Nebraska defensive back John Starkebaum's fancy.

Weekend Sports Calendar

Today

Sunday

Eubanks' Idea Good on Paper, Better on the Field

By Steve Love
Of The Tribune Sports Staff

Moore 40-7 Victim

Hale Advances To Semifinals

By Bill Harper
Assistant Sports Editor

Skiatook, Bristow Fall

Dream Ends For Bulldogs

ALL EYES ON THE BALL—Oklahoma University's Tinker Owens (11) and Nebraska defensive back Mark Heydorff (22) have their sights on a pass. Davis goes Friday in the final quarter of OU's 27-0 victory over the Huskers.

Mounds 'Passes' Inola 21-12

Ada Outlasts Warriors 17-15

Tigers Hike Ticket Prices

Webster Finds Fire Too Late

By Jim Carley
Of The Tribune Sports Staff

Oilers Seek to Extend Streak Against Wings

By Jim Monden

Three Named

CHAPTER 9 'FREE THE PUB'

"Barry says Tinker has charisma, but Wendell says that's alright — he'll be able to play by Saturday."

— Locker room story during last week of season.

Preparing for the last game of the season, the "state championship" against Oklahoma State, is always a season within a season at Oklahoma. Switzer's dilemma was that while he could tap the disdain his players had for the Aggies he also had a team that was wrung out from its traditional showdown with Nebraska. Tinker's attitude typified that of the team: "I can't stand those Cowboys. I love to play them and beat their ass. But it feels like the season ended last week."

Switzer's approach, therefore, was to play it loose and lighthearted all week. He

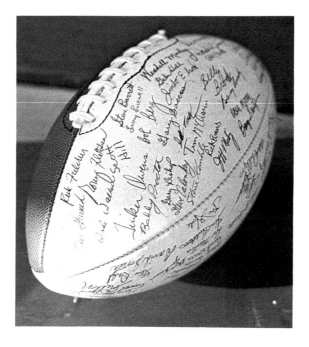

cheerfully received his post-season memento from the scrub team. And he laughed at the story being told on Wendell Mosley, the good-natured backfield coach: "Barry says that Tinker has charisma. But Wendell says it's alright — he'll be able to play Saturday."

Yet Switzer never let his team lose focus on its season-long goal — the first undefeated season at OU since 1956. He reminded them about the humiliation of losing to a rival that had beaten Oklahoma only twice since 1945. But the clincher came when he reached back into the season for something that even Knute Rockne may have overlooked.

After the Colorado victory, the Sooners were a little over-enthusiastic in celebrating at the Pub, and a fifth-string player was arrested and subsequently thrown off the team. Irate, Switzer called a special team meeting and placed the Pub off-limits. "I've never seen him so mad," Tinker recalled.

Now it was Thursday, the last week of the season, and Switzer was addressing his team out on the field at the end of practice.

"Everybody knows that the game this week is for the state championship," he said. "And we could still win the national championship — if we're lucky."

He paused. "Now if these stakes aren't high enough, I've got something I know that will give you real motivation. We're going to play Saturday — to Free the Pub!" He grinned, and a great cheer roared up from the players.

"Hell, they'll beat those Cowboys by 50 points now," cracked Switzer as he headed for the dressing room.

Barry Switzer receives a momento from the Sooner scrubs to go with his Coach of the Year honors from The Sporting News.

The Sooners unwind as OU "Termites" give out their post-season "awards" following one practice. Below, Jeff Mabry poses as Brent Blackman, the Oklahoma State quarterback. Jim Stanley is the OSU coach.

During the final week of practice, players were autographing Nebraska game balls.

A former Oklahoma coach once made a speech to his third and fourth-string players, stressing how important their morale was to the team's success. "Don't be termites," he said. "Don't eat away at the foundation with a bunch of bickering and complaining." The name "termites" caught on for Sooner scrubs ever since.

After the last practice of the year they give out their traditional awards. This season the "Little Termite of the Year" was Lucious Selmon, the "baddest" middle guard in the country. And the "Big Termite" was Barry Switzer. The coaches also presented battered old deflated footballs to the best "termite" players.

During the week the coaches even pulled tricks on one another. One afternoon Larry Lacewell climbed into Switzer's locker, ready to pounce on the coach when he came in to dress for practice. Except that Vince Larsen, a hefty broadcaster, came into the room, plopped down in front of Switzer's locker and began talking with the other coaches. They could barely restrain their laughter, knowing Lacewell was trapped inside, and he was too embarrassed to tap on the door and say, "Let me out."

Finally Switzer came into the room and Larsen moved. But the coach stood there a moment, deep in concentration, and abruptly left for practice without ever going to his locker.

A prankster unrewarded, Lacewell walked the rest of the day slightly stooped.

To everyone's merriment, scrubs George Davis and Steve Kunkle mimic sideline antics of the OU coaches.

Following the Friday night pre-game movie in Oklahoma City (Clint Eastwood enjoined the chase on motorcycle in "Magnum Force"), players including Billy Brooks here emerged to find the joking Switzer revving up on the sidewalk.

T alking to a reporter before Saturday's kickoff, Switzer pointed out one aspect of the OU-OSU rivalry that works against the Sooners. "Oklahoma State always gets ready to play us," he said. "They will come out wild-eyed and fired-up. The reason is, they hate us. Our kids were recruited by both schools, so when they chose Oklahoma, they didn't have any animosity against Oklahoma State. But probably 60 or 70 per cent of their squad didn't have a choice because we wouldn't offer them a scholarship. We looked on them as second-class athletes. So you can just feel this hatred they have. They call us the 'tea sippers'."

Nevertheless, Oklahoma won handily, 45-18, and would again wind up as the second ranked team in the country. The brilliant running tandem of Joe Washington (1,173) and Waymon Clark (1,014) marked only the third time in college history that two players on one team rushed for over 1,000 yards in the same season.

Switzer addresses his team at halftime (above). Right, Tinker beats All-American Alvin Brown on a sideine reception.

138

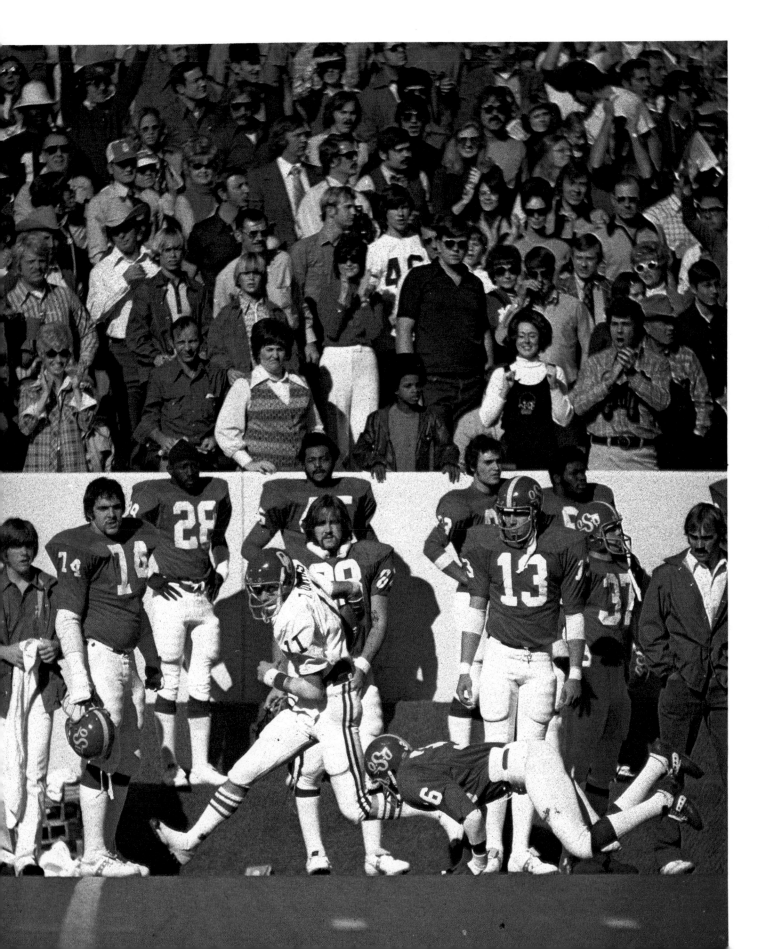

The season ends for Tinker when he is stunned by this shot to the helmet and has to be led off the field. Afterwards, he couldn't remember the incident.

Back in the spring Tinker had been voted by league players as the prospective All-Big Eight split receiver. But in post-season balloting by sportswriters he didn't even receive honorable mention.

"You can't blame them," said Tinker, after snaring four passes against Oklahoma State. "I only caught five passes in the five games before today. But I'm still looking forward to being the first team All-Big 8 receiver, even though we're not a passing team. There's a lot of personal pride as far as getting that. The Big 8 is the best football conference in the nation. If you're the best here, you're the best in the country, the way I look at it."

Tinker finished the year with 18 receptions for 472 yards, or 26.2 yards a catch. (He averaged 31.6 as a frosh.) Brooks caught 12 passes for 310 yards and a 25.8 average. As a team, the Sooners averaged a remarkable 24.1 yards each time a pass was completed, just below the NCAA record.

By season's end, Tinker wasn't overly happy about sharing playing time with Brooks but he was adjusting. A long talk with Don Duncan one afternoon had boosted his morale. Tinker recalled, "He said he saw how hard I worked my butt off in practice, and that Brooks wouldn't start ahead of me unless I just laid down and quit."

All things considered, had the season been fun for Tinker? "Yeh, it's been enjoyable," he said. "It's been frustrating compared to last year. But shoot, I don't see how you can keep from enjoying a year when you haven't lost a football game and you win the Big 8.

"I wouldn't mind if we had a bowl game, especially Alabama (then the No. 1 team). But we've played 11 games and everybody's getting pretty tired of it all."

More Sooners were injured against Oklahoma State than in any other game of the season: Rod Shoate (ankle), Randy Hughes (knee) and Durwood Keeton (mild concussion).

A zealous Sooner fan comes down on the field for Switzer's autograph . . .

. . . But her kiss was reserved for Tinker.

There were still a couple of minutes to play when a silver-blonde woman climbed out of the Oklahoma rooting section and trotted over to the OU bench. Squeezed into an Oklahoma-red pants suit, she pushed her way through players and coaches until she stood next to Barry Switzer at the edge of the field. He was still absorbed in the game and gave her only a cursory glance — then a sudden double take.

"Could I get your autograph?" she asked sweetly. Switzer smiled, bemused by this interloper, and signed her program. Then she headed straight for Tinker, who stood there grinning, holding his helmet, and planted a big kiss on him. Mission accomplished, she scurried back up into the stands.

"My God," Tinker said, "I hope Terri didn't see that."

Moments later the gun sounded, ending 14 weeks of football for Tinker Owens. The Sooners would enjoy themselves that night, celebrating the liberation of the Pub, and feasting on trays of gulf shrimp, cheese, barbequed ham and turkey. Yet everyone had a slightly hollow feeling. "I know this was a great team," said Switzer, "but we'll never know how great, without playing in a bowl."

Sunday afternoon there was no game film to watch, no running to loosen aching muscles. That evening, after Terri had returned to Miami, Tinker picked up a pizza and came back to his room, ever so reluctantly, to study for an important test on Monday.

"Damn accounting," he muttered.

Acknowledgements

Additional photography of the Oklahoma-Nebraska game by Brian Lanker, James Richardson and Jeff Jacobsen.

For the use of selected photographs previously published by Sports Illustrated, copyright 1973, Time, Inc.

For assistance to John Keith, sports information director of the University of Oklahoma; Tom Vanderschmidt, deputy picture editor of Sports Illustrated; Howard Neumann, host, "The Barry Switzer Show."

For the use of pages of the sports sections of November 24, 1973; The Tulsa Daily World, The Tulsa Tribune, The Oklahoma Journal and the Oklahoma Publishing Company, publishers of The Oklahoma City Times and The Daily Oklahoman, copyright 1973.

For quotations used in "Meat on the Hoof," by Gary Shaw, St. Martin's Press, New York, 1972; "Saturday's Children" by Dan Jankins, Little and Brown Company, 1970.

The 'SOONER' text was set in 12-point Times Roman, the captions in 8-point Optima, the headlines hand set in Woodstock Black. The book was printed by lithography on 80-pound dull enamel.